Spiritual Classics
from the
Early Church

Earthly longings have been crucified in me;
there is no spark of desire for mundane things,
but only a murmur of living water
that whispers within me 'Come to the Father'.

IGNATIUS OF ANTIOCH

Spiritual Classics

from the

Early Church

AN ANTHOLOGY

compiled and introduced by

ROBERT ATWELL OSB

National Society/Church House Publishing

National Society/Church House Publishing
Church House
Great Smith Street
London
SW1P 3NZ

ISBN: 978-0-7151-4341-4

First published in 1995 by The National Society and Church House Publishing

Cover design by Leigh Hurlock
Page design and typesetting by Church House Publishing
Print arranged by Indeprint Print Production Services
Printed in Finland by WSOY

CONTENTS

To my parents

ACKNOWLEDGEMENTS

I am grateful to many for the help, advice and encouragement that has made possible the production of this anthology. My first debt of gratitude is to my Community for their generosity in giving me time to do the work, and for their support and patience throughout. I am also grateful to Dr Sue Gillingham and Sr Benedicta Ward SLG, whose wise criticisms and advice have been invaluable.

Where good modern English translations of the Fathers have been made available, I have used these. In this context, I am grateful to the following for copyright permission to use extracts from their publications:

Cowley Publications, for excerpts from *Be Friends of God: Spiritual Reading from Gregory the Great*, translated and selected by John Leinenweber, 1990;

Mowbrays, for excerpts from *The Sayings of the Desert Fathers: The Alphabetical Collection*, translated by Benedicta Ward, 1975/83;

The Liturgical Press, Collegeville, for an extract from *The Life and Miracles of St Benedict*, translated by Odo Zimmermann and Benedict Avery;

Charles Scribner's Sons, an imprint of Macmillan Publishing Company for excerpts from *From Glory to Glory: Texts from Gregory of Nyssa*, edited by Jean Danielou, translated by Herbert Mursurillo, 1961;

New City, for excerpts from Olivier Clement, (ET) *The Roots of Christian Mysticism*, 1993; and *Born to New Life*, edited and selected by Oliver Davies, translated by Tim Witherow, 1991;

Oxford University Press, for two excerpts from *Augustine: Confessions*, translated by Henry Chadwick, 1991;

Paulist Press, for excerpts from John Cassian, *Conferences*, translated by Colm Luibheid, 1985; Athanasius, *The Life of Antony*, translated by Robert Gregg, 1980; Gregory of Nyssa, *The Life of Moses*, translated by Abraham Malherbe and Everett Ferguson, 1978;

Penguin Books Ltd, for excerpts from *Augustine: City of God*, translated by Henry Bettenson, 1972;

SLG Press, for excerpts from *The Wisdom of the Desert Fathers: The Anonymous Series*, translated by Benedicta Ward, 1986.

Where no source for an English translation is acknowledged at the end of an extract, the version is my own, sometimes based on an existing nineteenth-century translation but freely revised in the light of current knowledge of the text and into a more modern idiom. The translations are not offered as original pieces of scholarship. Sometimes, to avoid technical language, it has also been necessary to use informal paraphrase, but never (I hope) in such a way as to be inaccurate or misleading. I have attempted to render the Fathers not simply in good, modern English, but also in inclusive language. This is a departure from the majority of translations currently available, but consonant with the demands of a contemporary readership. Occasionally, this has necessitated minor modifications to a text, but where these occur it is noted. I have made little attempt, however, in the extracts from *The Rule of St Benedict* to modify his language to include women: Benedict wrote for monks and it seemed artificial to pretend otherwise. As a member of a Benedictine community of monks and nuns, I hope I may be excused this eccentricity.

Robert Atwell OSB
Burford Priory

ABBREVIATIONS

ACW   Ancient Christian Writers: The Works of the Fathers in Translation; ed. J. Quasten and J.C. Plumpe, Newman Press/ Paulist Press, New York, 1946-

CCSL   Corpus Christianorum Series Latina, Turnhout, Brepols, 1953 -

cf.   compare

CSEL   Corpus Scriptorum Ecclesiasticorum Latinorum, Vienna, 1866 -

CUP   Cambridge University Press, Cambridge and London

DLT   Darton, Longman and Todd

ET   English translation

LCC   The Library of Christian Classics, Westminster Press, Philadelphia; SCM, London, 1953-66

NRSV   New Revised Standard Version, 1989

OUP   Oxford University Press, New York & Oxford

PG   *Patrologiae cursus completus: series graeca*, 161 vols, ed. J.P. Migne, Paris, 1857-66

PL   *Patrologiae cursus completus: series latina*, 221 vols, ed. J.P. Migne, Paris, 1844-6

NPNF   The Nicene and Post-Nicene Library of the Fathers, general editors Schaff and Wace, New York, 1887-92; Oxford, 1890-1900; reprinted Michigan, 1983-

op.cit.   the work previously cited

RB   *The Rule of St Benedict*

SC   Sources Chrétiennes, Les Editions du Cerf, Paris, 1942-

SPCK   Society for Promoting Christian Knowledge

vol.   volume

AUTHOR'S NOTE

Biblical annotations refer to the NRSV. In a few cases readers may observe a variation between a writer's version and most modern translations. This is particularly the case with the Latin Fathers such as Augustine who used a Latin version of the Septuagint (the Greek Old Testament, often abbreviated as LXX) in which certain translations of the original Hebrew are different.

The Fathers also numbered the psalms according to the Septuagint, a numeration adopted by the 'Old Latin Versions' used by Cyprian and Augustine, and the Latin *Vulgate* compiled by Jerome and completed c.404, which became the standard text for the Western Church. Unfortunately, this numbering does not always correspond to that of the Hebrew Psalter on which the *Book of Common Prayer*, the Liturgical Psalter included in the *Alternative Service Book*, and most modern translations are based. To minimize confusion, therefore, references to the psalms in this anthology follow the Hebrew numeration, except where titles of individual works are concerned, and where this occurs, the alternative numeration is noted.

Christians, like the Jews, assumed the Davidic authorship of all the psalms, and therefore received them as uniquely authoritative. They interpreted them as if spoken by David, and believed them to be uttered through a spirit of prophecy, hence the frequent reference of the Fathers to the author of the psalms as 'the prophet' or as 'David'. In this anthology the former designation is rendered 'the psalmist' to avoid confusion for the modern reader, except where a translation under copyright has been used.

The Fathers also followed the convention of designating St Paul as the author of the Epistle to the Hebrews, and of designating him simply as 'the apostle'. In this anthology these designations are rendered as 'Paul the apostle' or just 'Paul'.

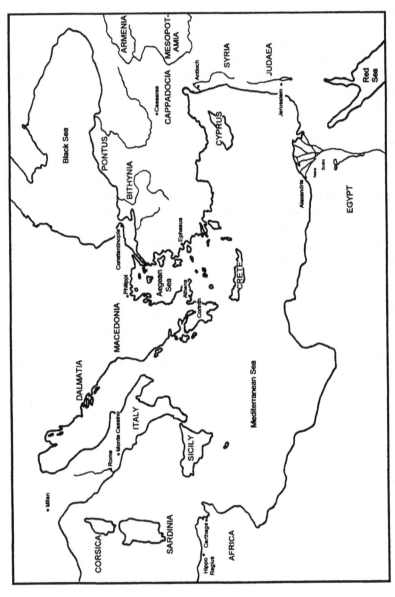

The ancient world in the early Christian centuries, showing locations referred to in the text.

Introduction

E vagrius of Pontus, a fourth-century theologian wrote: 'If you are a
theologian you will pray truly; and if you pray truly you are a
theologian.'[1] Were Evagrius alive today he would be perplexed by
the modern tendency to compartmentalise human experience. As Christians
and as a society we need to recover that balance of mind and heart celebrated
by earlier generations in which life and thought, and prayer and belief
interact freely, and are not kept in watertight compartments. At the end of
the second century an unknown Christian wrote a short treatise to an
intellectual and cultured pagan called Diognetus in an attempt to explain to
him what it meant to be a Christian living in the world. He wrote as follows:

Christians are not distinguishable from other people by nationality or
language or the way they dress. They do not live in cities reserved to
themselves; they do not speak a special dialect; there is nothing
eccentric about their way of life. Their beliefs are not the invention
of some sharp, inquisitive mind, nor are they like some, slaves of this
or that school of thought. They are distributed among Greek and
non-Greek cities alike, according to their human lot. They conform
to local usage in their dress, diet, and manner of life. Nevertheless in
their communities they do reveal some extraordinary and undeniably
paradoxical attitudes. They live each in his or her own native country,
but they are like pilgrims in transit. They play their full part as citizens
and are content to submit to every burden as if they were resident
aliens. For them, every foreign country is home, and every homeland
is foreign territory.

They marry like everyone else. They beget children, but they do
not abandon them at birth. They will share their table with you, but
not their marriage bed. They are in the world, but they refuse to
conform to the ways of the world. They pass their days on earth, but
their citizenship is in heaven. They obey the established laws, but in
their way of life transcend all laws. They show love to all people, but
all persecute them. They are misunderstood and condemned; they are

11

killed and yet gain life. Poor themselves, they make many rich. Materially they possess nothing, and yet they possess everything. They are despised, and yet in this contempt they discover glory; they are slandered, and yet are vindicated. They counter false accusations with blessings, and abuse with courtesy. In spite of the good they do, they are punished as criminals, but in the face of such punishment rejoice like those given a new lease of life. Jews denounce them as heretics, and Greeks harass them with the threat of persecution; and in spite of all this ill-treatment, no one can produce grounds for hostility. In a word, what the soul is to the body, Christians are to the world.[2]

Today Christians continue to bear witness to the claims of Christ and the values of the Gospel in lives of prayer, mutual love and service, and in a concern for an integrity in national and international affairs that mirrors the justice of God. As an institution, however, the Church (at least in Britain) is hesitant. It finds itself functioning in a secular society which, if not exactly pagan, is certainly materialistic, one in which Christians often feel themselves to be 'resident aliens'. The moral and spiritual consensus that had informed and invigorated the culture of European society is crumbling, and with it the Church's right to speak with authority on a variety of issues. Christians find themselves living and working in situations where they share few agreed moral parameters with their contemporaries. In spite of the frequent calls addressed by politicians to the Church for moral leadership, late twentieth century Europeans tend to be either apathetic or overtly hostile to Christianity. As a result the Christian community invariably finds itself on the defensive, easily demoralised by its progressive marginalisation in public affairs, or depressed by aggressive negative coverage in the media. Typically, Christianity is portrayed as an optional leisure activity, rarely as a life-force.

In the face of apathy or contempt, the temptation for any minority group is to retreat into the relative safety and security of the ghetto or club. The option is as real for the Church today as it was for the Church in the second and third centuries. And yet when one reads texts from the early Church such as the one quoted above, what comes across is not a ghetto mentality, but self-confidence, openness and engagement with the reality of the world (however bleak), and above all, a profound confidence in God and his purposes. Christians believed themselves to be 'the soul of the world'; they understood their prayer as creating the spiritual oxygen that could purify the stale, polluted atmosphere of the world to make possible the salvation of humankind. As the Church enters the third millennium, if it is to fulfil its vocation of embodying and proclaiming the good news of Jesus Christ, then it is imperative that it renews its self-understanding as the sacrament of God's presence in and to his world. It needs to recover its own soul if it is to have one to offer the world it seeks both to serve and to leaven.

This anthology of readings from the early Church (which is the first in a series of classics of Christian spirituality) is concerned to assist in this process of spiritual renewal, and in the allied task of recovering that balance of mind and heart in theological reflection which in the past has contributed so significantly to the vitality of the Church. The purpose of the anthology is thus two-fold: it is concerned to help people reflect upon their faith in the company of Christian men and women whose intimacy with God gave to their lives and writings an authority which is both compelling and challenging; and it is concerned to encourage people in their discipleship and prayer. The purpose is both educational and devotional.

Irenaeus, writing at the end of the second century, said that 'The glory of God is a human being fully alive, and the life of humanity consists in the vision of God.'[3] In this selection of writings we encounter not only people's vision of God, but also their understanding of what it means to be human, to be fully alive. The choice of authors and the material selected are entirely personal: here are texts that have inspired me in my pilgrimage of faith. But the range of potential material for a patristic anthology is vast. Cyril of Alexandria said that 'Prayer is keeping company with God'.[4] I have assembled extracts from seven authors, together with a selection of the stories and sayings of the Desert Fathers and Mothers, to show how some of our earliest Christian forebears 'kept company with God'. Individually, the writers represent a broad spectrum of spirituality; but collectively, they constitute a powerful witness to the coherence and continuity of the Christian tradition as it emerged from the era of the apostles and passed to the medieval Church. They are drawn equally from what is customarily called 'Eastern' Christianity (predominantly Greek speaking), and from 'Western' Christianity (predominantly Latin speaking). One writer was martyred for his faith, one died in exhaustion in the ignominy of exile, others died peacefully in their beds. Some were bishops, one was a distinguished abbot, one was Pope of Rome: all were noted for their pastoral sensitivity. One was married, one had a common law wife and had had a child by her, others were celibate; some were monks and nuns living in the deserts or mountains, consciously repudiating the decadence of society. Whoever they were, whatever the circumstances of their lives, all were people who were 'fully alive', people who saw life whole and interpreted their own existence and the world in which they were set in the light of the death and resurrection of Jesus Christ.

The literature represented spans over five centuries of theological exploration. It includes sermons, commentaries on Scripture, theological treatises, personal letters, lectures, prayers, stories and pithy sayings. Some extracts will seem astonishingly modern, others more obscure. There is a vitality and variety of thought in the Fathers which can surprise the modern reader. But it is a mistake to be nostalgic about the early Christian centuries or to project onto them an idealism of uniformity and tranquillity. Our Christian forebears knew conflict and theological controversy as much as we do. It is only by reading these texts in their context of vigour and turbulence that a wisdom and an authentic spirituality can be discerned which will be enriching, and potentially healing of our ecclesiastical divisions. It is easy to be critical of the Christian tradition; it is less easy to understand and appreciate the past in its own right, and allow the tradition to interrogate us, to expose our misconceptions or disturb the mediocrity of our discipleship. In our current human and ecclesiastical fragmentation we need to plumb the wells of Christian spirituality and to re-appropriate our common heritage.

Classical Anglicanism has always appealed not simply to Scripture, but also to the witness of the undivided Church of the first Christian centuries. In the interaction of the three-fold cord of Scripture, Tradition and Reason, there is a way of doing theology that is both distinctive and distinguished. The current reality, however, is that most Anglicans (doubtless like many Christians in other traditions) have only a minimal knowledge of the Fathers. I offer this anthology to these readers in particular, and to all who want to begin to explore the Fathers, in the hope that by introducing them to something of the richness of our heritage, hearts will be enlarged and minds expanded.

NOTES

1   *On Prayer*, 61.
2   *Letter to Diognetus*, 5; SC 33.
3   *Adversus haereses*, 4,20.7.
4   *Commentary on St John's Gospel*, 4,4.

1

Cyprian
THE PRAYER OF THE CHURCH

'We are born in the womb of the Church;
we are nourished by her milk;
and we are animated by her Spirit.'

ON THE UNITY OF THE CHURCH

It is difficult for those familiar with the landscape and peoples of North Africa to comprehend just what demographic and cultural changes have occurred over the last two thousand years. Before the relentless advance of the Sahara desert, North Africa was so productive that it was known as the granary of the Roman Empire. In the second and third centuries the region had more Christian bishoprics than virtually any other province. Today a visitor will encounter a predominantly Islamic culture.

How Christianity arrived on the shores of North Africa remains one of the unsolved riddles of history. It is possible that it came with Greek speaking migrants. It is possible that the first Christian converts in Africa were from the Jewish community; but the theory, although attractive, remains unproven.[1] The first documentary evidence for the presence of Christianity does not occur until 180 with the martyrdom of a group of Christians from a small town that has never been located. It is also about this time that the first African Christian writers emerged. They were Latin speaking; and in marked contrast to their contemporaries in Alexandria who used philosophical vocabulary, these theologians preferred terminology and concepts drawn from Roman law to communicate their ideas. They were also more pastoral and pragmatic in their writing, and generally less highbrow. Prominent among them was Thascius Caecilianus Cyprianus.

Cyprian was born into a rich and cultured pagan family sometime between 200 and 210, probably in Carthage, the foremost city of the region. He was a celebrated orator, but in about 246 at the age of forty he became a Christian. His conversion was the sensation of the city. He sold the greater part of his possessions for the benefit of the poor, devoted himself to the study of the Scriptures, and was soon ordained priest. In his treatise *To Donatus* he described how he had been a 'stranger to truth and to the light'[2] but that, thanks to his upbringing, he had received a good literary education which he now intended to put at the disposal of the Church. He described how the power of the Spirit, flowing from baptism and the sacramental life of the Church, together with reflection upon the Scriptures, had effected a radical transformation in his life.

Cyprian had all the qualities of a born leader. He was eloquent; he had a sharp mind; he was shrewd. His pastoral ability also quickly emerged, and in 249 he was elected bishop 'by the judgement of God and the voice of the people.'[3] Within weeks of his ordination, however, persecution broke out under the emperor Decius. Cyprian went underground, keeping in touch with his flock by letter.[4]

In Carthage, as in Rome, the Church was decimated. Large numbers of Christians lapsed from their faith; some gave in to the demand to offer sacrifice to the statue of the emperor; others bribed the imperial police, secretly purchasing false documents which certified that they had performed the requisite sacrifice in order to escape imprisonment and death. In 251 the persecution stopped, and Cyprian emerged from hiding. When he returned to Carthage he was confronted by a divided and disillusioned Christian community. On the one hand there were the rigorists, determined to stop at all costs the readmission to communion of apostate Christians. On the other hand there were those who favoured a general amnesty. To add to the confusion, there were the 'confessors' (those Christians who had confessed their faith and managed to survive torture or imprisonment) busy reconciling the lapsed on their own authority and by virtue of the merits of the martyrs. The notion had grown up that these heroes of the Church were empowered to dispose of their superfluous merit to weaker brethren who might thus gain remission of the consequences of their failure. They were quick to ridicule Cyprian, accusing him of cowardice. In the face of mounting chaos, Cyprian had no alternative but to assert his episcopal authority decisively.[5] He enacted a moderate policy which sought to care for the sinner without trivialising the sin. He decided that the lapsed were to be restored to the fellowship of the Church, but only after suitable delay. Each case was to be considered on its own merits, and penance was to be proportionate to the seriousness of the offence.

Undergirding Cyprian's pastoral sensitivity was a strong vision of the Church as God's instrument for bringing the reconciliation wrought in Christ to the world. In 251 at the Council of Carthage, he read his treatise *On the Unity of the Church* to the unanimous approval of the African bishops. It was Cyprian's view that 'outside the Church salvation is granted to no one.'[6] And in another celebrated phrase he declared: 'No one can have God as Father who does not also have the Church as mother.'[7] In this treatise three images predominate: the Church is mother, ark, and virgin-bride. Cyprian's strong feminine imagery corresponded with the high theology of baptism in early Christian thought. It reflected a need to express the spiritual reality of what had taken place in the sacrament of rebirth and it underscored the nurturing role of the Church. Cyprian pictured the Church bringing forth into the world a new breed of humanity. He characterised the waters of baptism as waters of a womb, with Mother Church labouring over her infants: 'We are born in her womb, nourished by her milk, animated by her Spirit.'[8]

Not surprisingly it is also in the Church that the Christian learns how to pray, and finds the grace to call God 'Father'. For Cyprian, the Lord's Prayer is central to Christian spirituality, as will be apparent in the selection of extracts from his treatise *On the Lord's Prayer* that follows. The Church is a praying community gathered around its bishop; the eucharist reveals and cements its unity. But the Church is also the ark of salvation and the virgin-bride of Christ, and as such it demands of its members a love and a fidelity that admit no compromise.

Persecution was no sooner over when plague broke out in Carthage. Trouble threatened afresh, people holding the 'atheists' (i.e. Christians) responsible. Cyprian managed to deflect the unrest by organising extensive charitable relief, and in his treatise *On the Mortality Rate* attempted to give comfort to the grieving populace. During his episcopate he wrote on various problems that touched society in general. In *On Works and Almsgiving*, for example, he expressed his anger at the corruption and injustice in civic life; and in his treatise *On Patience* he discussed issues of peace and non-violence, and revealed a profound insight into the nature of suffering.

From the experience of persecution and its aftermath, however, Cyprian grasped the paramount importance of securing Christian unity if the Church was to survive and the Gospel to be proclaimed. In the face of competing claims to his authority, he also realised that the unity of the Church was dependent on the unity of its bishops. The local episcopate needed to work together much better if it was to be an effective sign of Christian unity. For Cyprian this also included their union with the apostolic see of Rome to which Carthage looked for support. For so convinced an exponent of unity, therefore, it must have come as a devastating blow in 255 to discover himself at loggerheads with Stephen, the Bishop of Rome. Stephen admitted the validity of the baptism administered by heretics and schismatics, whereas Cyprian denied it, and in this Cyprian was supported unanimously by his fellow-bishops in Africa. Sadly, the personal conflict between the two men was never resolved except by their deaths.

Persecution erupted again under the emperor Valerian. In Rome Stephen was the first to be executed in 256. In Carthage Cyprian was arrested, but to begin with only sent into exile. Two years later, however, on 14 September 258 he was condemned to death and beheaded. Earlier he had written an *Exhortation to Martyrdom* in which he had proclaimed it the duty of every Christian to bear public witness to Christ, even though this result in imprisonment, torture or death. The thrust of Cyprian's thinking exercises a powerful critique on much contemporary theology which focuses on the problems of human existence in this present age. By contrast, Cyprian always saw this world as provisional. His gaze was fixed on an eternal horizon, upon God and his coming reign in which evil would have no hold. His theology continues to resonate with many, but particularly with those Christians for whom suffering, disease and an early death are commonplace.

In his martyrdom, Cyprian consciously witnessed to the eternal dimension of the Christian faith. His death set a unique seal of authority upon a life which, by any standard, was heroic.

Born again

If you are speaking in court, before the assembly or the senate, a lavish and extravagant eloquence is appropriate. But before God, our master, the absolute sincerity of our speech is supported not by our arguments but rather by our actions. And so accept these words that have power rather than facility and are designed not to win over a popular audience by their fancy turns of phrase, but to preach the mercy of God by the naked simplicity of the truth. Accept that which has been sincerely felt rather than merely learned, that which has not been laboriously accumulated over the course of a long apprenticeship but seized in an instant by a sudden act of grace.

Once I lay in darkness and in the depths of night and was tossed to and fro in the waves of the turbulent world, uncertain of the correct way to go, ignorant of my true life and a stranger to the light of truth. At that time and on account of the life I then led, it seemed difficult to believe what divine mercy promised for my salvation, namely, that someone could be born again and to a new life by being immersed in the healing waters of baptism. It was difficult to believe that though I would remain the same man in bodily form, my heart and mind would be transformed.

How was it possible, I thought, that a change could be great enough to strip away in a single moment the innate hardness of our nature? How could the habits acquired over the course of many years disappear, since these are so deeply rooted within us? If someone is used to fine feasts and lavish banquets, how can they learn restraint? If someone is used to dressing conspicuously in gold and purple, how can they cast them aside for ordinary simple clothes? Someone who loves the trappings of public office cannot become an anonymous private person. Anyone who is attended by great crowds of supporters and is honoured by a dense entourage of obsequious attendants would consider solitude a punishment. While temptation still holds us fast, we are seduced by wine, inflated with pride, inflamed by anger, troubled by greed, goaded by cruelty, enticed by ambition and cast headlong by lust.

These were my frequent thoughts. For I was held fast by the many sins of my life from which it seemed impossible for me to extricate myself. Thus I yielded to my sins which clung fast to me. Since I despaired of improvement I took an indulgent view of my faults and regarded them as if they were slaves born in my house.

But after the life-giving water of baptism came to my rescue and washed away the stain of my former years and poured into my cleansed and purified heart the light which comes from above, and after I had drunk in the Heavenly Spirit and was made a new man by a second birth, then amazingly what I had previously doubted became clear to me. What had been hidden was revealed. What had been dark became light. What previously had seemed impossible now seemed possible. What was in me of the guilty flesh now confessed it was earthly. What was made alive in me by the Holy Spirit was now quickened by God.

To Donatus, 2-4; ET Tim Witherow, *Born to New Life*, pp.26-8.

Pray with humility and integrity

When we pray, our words and petitions must be properly ordered, and our attitude should be receptive and modest. Our bodily posture and our tone of voice should reflect the fact that we are standing in the presence of God. Loud people end up shouting noisily at God, but a more modest person will pray in a quiet manner. Moreover, in his teaching on the subject the Lord himself has told us to pray in secret, in hidden and private places, even in our very bedrooms.[9] This way of praying is best suited to our faith in order that we may know that God is present everywhere, that he hears and sees everything, and that in the fullness of his majesty, he penetrates even hidden and secret places. For it is written: 'I am a God nearby, and not a God far off. Who can hide in secret places so that I cannot see them? Do I not fill heaven and earth?'[10] And again: 'The eyes of the Lord are in every place, keeping watch on the evil and the good.'[11] . . .

Hannah, who is a type of the Church in the first book of Samuel, is faithful and obedient in these things.[12] It is evident that she prayed to God not with loud petitions, but silently and modestly in the secret places of her heart. She uttered a hidden prayer, but with obvious faith. She spoke not with her voice, but with her heart knowing that the Lord hears such prayer. She truly received because she asked in the right way. As Holy Scripture records of her: 'Hannah was praying silently; only her lips moved, but her voice was not heard,'[13] and the Lord heard her. We also read in the Psalms: 'Speak in the silence of your hearts, and ponder your sins upon your bed.'[14] The Holy Spirit, moreover, suggests and teaches the same thing in the words of Jeremiah: 'But in your heart say, "It is you, O Lord, whom we must worship."'[15]

My friends, let no worshipper be ignorant of how the tax gatherer, as opposed to the pharisee, prayed in the temple. The tax gatherer would not even raise his eyes to heaven let alone pray with his hands lifted up ostentatiously. Instead he struck his breast and admitted the sins that lay hidden within, begging the help of the divine mercy. Whereas the pharisee was rather pleased with himself, it was in fact the tax gatherer who was deemed holy because again, he asked God in the right way. He did not place his hope of salvation in an imagined innocence – indeed, before God no one can claim innocence. Rather he confessed his sins and prayed humbly, and the God who attends to the humble heard his prayer.

On the Lord's Prayer, 4-6.

Our Father

Above all else, the Teacher of peace and the Master of unity does not wish us to pray individualistically or selfishly as if we are concerned only about ourselves. We do not say: 'My Father in heaven', or 'Give me today my daily bread.' Nor does anyone pray simply for their own sins to be forgiven, or request that he or she alone be not led into temptation or be delivered from evil. Christian prayer is public and offered for all. When we pray it is not as an individual but as a united people, for we are indeed all one. God, who is the Teacher of prayer and peace, taught us peace. He wishes each of us to pray for all, just as he carries us all in himself . . .

What profound mysteries, my dear brothers and sisters, are contained in the Lord's Prayer! How many and how great they are! They are expressed in few words but overflow in an abundance of virtue. Nothing is left out; everything is comprehended in these few petitions. It is a compendium of spiritual teaching. 'This is how you must pray,' says the Lord, 'Our Father in heaven.' The new man or woman, who has been born again and restored to God through grace, says 'Father' at the beginning of all prayer because they are already beginning to be a son or daughter. As Scripture says: 'He came among his own and his own people did not accept him. But to all who received him, who believed in his name, he gave power to become children of God.'[16] Thus whoever has believed in his name and has been made a child of God should begin from this point to give thanks and to acknowledge their adoption, and learn to call God their heavenly Father . . . None of us would presume to call God our Father had not Christ himself taught us to pray in this way. We must realise then, dearest brothers and sisters, that if we are to call God 'Father', we ought to behave like sons and daughters of God, so that just as we are delighted to have God as our Father, so equally he can take delight in us his children.

On the Lord's Prayer, 8-9,11.

Hallowed be your name

We should live as temples of God that it may be plain to all that God dwells in us. It is important that our conduct should not degenerate and become unworthy of the Spirit. Rather let we who have set out to be heavenly and spiritual, entertain only heavenly and spiritual thoughts and behaviour. For the Lord God himself has declared: 'I will glorify those who glorify me; but those that despise me, I shall despise.'[17] The blessed apostle Paul has likewise stated in one of his letters: 'You are not your own. You were bought at a price; therefore, glorify God in your body.'[18]

[In the Lord's Prayer] we go on to say: 'Hallowed be your name.' We are not envisaging that God will be made holy by our prayers: we are asking rather that his holiness should shine in us. Anyway, by whom could God be sanctified since it is God himself who sanctifies? But observe that in Scripture it is also written: 'Be holy because I am holy.'[19] Thus it should be our earnest desire that we, who have been made holy in baptism, should continue to grow in what we have begun to be; and this we pray every day. We certainly need to be made holy daily because every day we sin, and every day we need to have those sins washed away. In this way we are engaged in a process that makes us ever more deeply sanctified.

On the Lord's Prayer, 11.

Your kingdom come

We pray 'Your kingdom come'. In this petition we are asking that the kingdom of God may be made present to us, just as we have already prayed that God's name may be made holy in us. For when has a time existed when God has not reigned? What has already existed with God can never cease to exist any more than it can be said to have had a beginning. It is for the coming of our kingdom, the kingdom that has been promised to us, that we are praying. That kingdom was rooted in us through the blood of Christ's passion. We have the privilege of being its first subjects, and we pray that we may reign with Christ, sharing in his sovereignty, as he has promised: 'Come, you blessed of my Father, inherit the kingdom that has been in preparation for you since the beginning of the world.'[20]

My dear brothers and sisters, it may be that Christ himself is the kingdom of God, he whom we desire each day to come, whose coming we crave to be accomplished. Since he is himself our resurrection because in him we rise again, so too he can be understood as the kingdom of God because it is in Christ that we are to reign. We do well to seek the kingdom of God, that is the kingdom of heaven, because there is also an earthly kingdom that beckons to us. Those who have renounced the world have already transcended its glitter and power. It is why in dedicating ourselves to God and to Christ, our desire should be not for earthly kingdoms, but heavenly. There is need for constant prayer and petition lest we fall away.

On the Lord's Prayer, 13.

Your will be done

When we pray 'Your will be done on earth as in heaven' we are not praying that God may accomplish what he wills, but that we may be able to do what God wills. For who can prevent God from doing what he wills? The reality of our situation is that it is we who are prevented from completely obeying God in our thoughts and deeds because of the activity of the devil. That is why we pray that we may will what God wills. If this is to happen we need God's goodwill, by which is meant his help and protection. Nobody is sufficiently strong, whatever their inner resources: it is only by the grace and mercy of God that we are saved.

Indeed, our Lord himself revealed the fragility of his humanity when he prayed: 'Father, if it is possible, let this cup pass me by.' And then he gave his disciples an example that they should do God's will and not their own when he went on to say: 'Nevertheless, not what I will but what you will.'[21] If the Son was obedient to the Father's will, how much more should we servants be concerned to do the will of our Master! . . .

It was the will of God, then, that Christ exemplified both in his deeds and in his teaching. It means humility in behaviour, constancy in faith, modesty in conversation, justice in deeds, mercy in judgements, discipline in morals. We should be incapable of doing wrong to anyone but able to bear patiently wrongs done to us. It requires that we live at peace with our brothers and sisters, loving God with our whole heart: loving him as our Father, fearing him as our God. It means preferring nothing whatever to Christ who preferred nothing to us. It means holding fast to his love and never letting go; standing by his cross bravely and fearlessly when his name and honour are challenged; exhibiting in our speech a conviction that will confess our faith. It also means that even under torture we sustain a confidence that will not surrender; and that in the face of death we allow our patience to be our crown. This is what is entailed in being a co-heir with Christ. This is what it means to accomplish the commandment of God, to fulfil the will of the Father.

On the Lord's Prayer, 14-15.

Give us today our daily bread

The petition 'Give us today our daily bread' may be understood both in a spiritual sense and in a literal sense: either interpretation is a God-given help to salvation. We recognise Christ to be the bread of life; and this bread is not common property, but belongs to us in a special way. Inasmuch as we have learned to say 'Our Father' and know God to be the Father of those who understand and believe; so also we have learned to call Christ 'our bread' because he is the food of those who are members of his body. Thus when we pray that we may receive this bread daily, we are asking that we who are incorporated into Christ may receive his eucharist daily as the food of our salvation. It is our prayer that we may not fall into some serious sin and be forced to abstain from communion because this would deprive us of the bread of heaven and separate us from the body of Christ . . .

But the petition may also be understood in a different way, that we who have renounced the world, and have forsaken its riches and pomp in an act of faith in God's grace, should only ever seek of God food and inner strength. In the Gospel the Lord has stated: 'None of you can be my disciple if you do not give up your possessions.'[22] Having renounced our possessions in obedience to the word of our Master, and begun a life of discipleship, we ought to pray for our food daily. And note, we are not to seek future needs because elsewhere the Lord also says: 'Do not worry about tomorrow, for tomorrow will bring worries of its own. Today's trouble is enough for today.'[23] With good reason then should we, as Christ's disciples, learn to ask simply for enough for each day. We are forbidden to ask for more. Indeed it is hypocritical and a contradiction in terms to be pleading at one moment for a long life in this world, and the next moment to be asking that the kingdom of God may come quickly! We should also recollect the words of Paul the blessed apostle who gives meaning and strength to our perseverance in hope and faith, when he says: 'We brought nothing into this world, and it is certain we can take nothing out of it; but if we have food and clothing, we should be content with these. But those who want to be rich fall into temptation and end up trapped by a multitude of senseless and harmful desires that plunge people into ruin and destruction. For the love of money is the root of all kinds of evil, and in their eagerness to be rich some have wandered away from the faith and pierced themselves with many pains.'[24] . . . Thus it is vital for us who follow Christ to learn not only how to pray, but also from the character of the prayer that Christ has taught us, the sort of people we are aiming to become through our prayer.

On the Lord's Prayer, 18-20.

Forgive us our sins

How necessary, how important and how salutary is the Lord's declaration to us that we are sinners when he compels us to pray on account of our sins! For in the process of asking for God's forgiveness, we become aware of the state of our conscience. Moreover we are commanded to pray daily for the forgiveness of our sins, and by so doing we are prevented from fantasising about our supposed innocence, or exalting our egos and thereby increasing the risk of our perdition. In his epistle John warns us as follows: 'If we say we have no sin, we deceive ourselves, and the truth is not in us. If we confess our sins, the Lord is faithful and just and will forgive us our sins.'[25] In his epistle John has combined two ideas: that we should seek pardon for our sins; and that when we ask for forgiveness, God may be trusted to grant it. This is why he states that God is faithful and true to his promise of forgiveness. He who taught us to pray on account of our sins and offences has promised that the fatherly mercy and pardon [of God] will be granted.

The Lord has clearly set forth the condition of such pardon; he has stated it as a law and expressed it as a covenant. We can only expect our sins to be forgiven according to the degree that we ourselves forgive those who sin against us. We are informed categorically that we will not be able to obtain what we ask for in respect of our sins unless we have acted ourselves in the same way to those who have sinned against us. Thus our Lord says in another place in Scripture: 'The measure you deal out will be dealt back to you.'[26] Similarly, the servant who refused to cancel his fellow servant's debt, in spite of having had his own debts cancelled by his master, was thrown into prison. Because he refused to be generous to his fellow servant, he forfeited the indulgence that had been shown to him by his master. These ideas Christ sets forth even more directly and stamps it with his own authority when he says: 'Whenever you stand praying, forgive, if you have anything against anyone; so that your Father in heaven may also forgive you your debts. But if you do not forgive, neither will your Father in heaven forgive you your debts.'[27] You will have no excuse on the day of judgement; you will be judged according to the sentence you have passed on others; whatever you have dealt out will be dealt back to you.

God commands us to be peacemakers, to live in harmony, and to be of one mind in his house. He warns those who have been born again to retain the character of their second birth. We who are the children of God must make the peace of God a reality in our lives; we who share in the one Spirit must also be of one heart and mind. God refuses the sacrifice of the quarrelsome, and instructs them to leave their gift before the altar, to go and be reconciled to their sister or brother. God is only pacified by prayer that is offered in a spirit of peace. So let our peace and fraternal harmony be the great sacrifice we offer God. In this way we become a people gathered into the unity of the Father, the Son, and the Holy Spirit.

On the Lord's Prayer, 22-23.

Lead us not into temptation

When we pray 'And lead us not into temptation', we should know that the Lord is teaching us inwardly. The words are there to reassure us that the adversary can do nothing against us because all is ultimately within the control of God. All power is from God. So in the temptations that assail us, we should consciously give our fear, our devotion and our obedience to God alone . . .

When we pray in these words we are put in touch with our vulnerability and inner weakness. We ask for help lest any should insolently exalt themselves, or become proud and conceited, or even hug to themselves the glory either of confessing their faith or of suffering [for Christ], as if it were all their own doing. The Lord himself has taught us to be humble when he said: 'Watch and pray that you enter not into temptation. The spirit is indeed willing, but the flesh is weak.'[28] When, however, we confess our need of God humbly and quietly, and surrender to God the glory that is properly his, then the prayer that is offered in the fear of God and to his honour will be met by his loving kindness.

On the Lord's Prayer, 25-26.

Deliver us from evil

At the end of various petitions, the Lord's Prayer concludes with a brief clause which in a few words neatly sums up our petitions and prayers. We conclude with the words 'But deliver us from evil,' an expression that includes everything that the enemy can devise against us in this world. We pray this in the conviction that God is a faithful and dependable protector who will give his help readily to all who ask and beg for it. Consequently, when we pray 'Deliver us from evil,' there is nothing left to ask for. When we have once asked for God's protection in the face of evil and secured it, then we stand secure and safe against any kind of machination of the devil and the evils of the world. For what is there in life to be afraid of when the Lord God is our protector?

You see, my brothers and sisters, how wonderful the Lord's Prayer is. It encompasses all that we could ask for in a few words ... For when our Lord Jesus Christ, the Word of God, came to this world, he gathered together both the learned and the uneducated, and set forth to every single human being, regardless of their sex or age, the precepts of salvation. He distilled his teaching in order that the memories of those receiving instruction in the way of heaven should not be intimidated, but might grasp easily the essentials of a simple faith. Thus, in his teaching about eternal life, he embraced the sacrament of life in a brevity which is both gracious and divine: 'And this is eternal life, that they may know you, the one true God, and Jesus Christ whom you have sent.'[29]

On the Lord's Prayer, 27-28.

Cyprian

Persevering in this vale of tears

Each one of us, when we are born into the inn of this world, begins our life with tears. Even though we be largely unconscious and ignorant of life, yet from the very first hours of birth, we know how to cry. It is as though our nature had foresight. From the moment of our birth, our inexperienced soul in its tears and wails testifies to the anxieties and burdens of human life, and the perils and storms that it is entering upon. For as long as this life lasts sweat and toil are part of the human condition. Nor is there any consolation for those who must endure them except patience.

While patience is helpful and necessary for everyone, it is especially appropriate for us who are more aware of the onslaught of the devil. We have to fight him in the front-line of battle every day, and end up exhausted by the tactics of our inveterate and skilful enemy. In addition to the various and continuous battles of temptation, we are also having to face in this time of persecution the loss of our family inheritance, the terror of imprisonment, being clamped in irons, and the loss of our lives either through the sword, or through being savaged by wild beasts, or by being burnt to death, or by being crucified. In short, every kind of torture and penalty is ours to be endured in faith and with the courage of patience . . .

Our Lord and Master gives us a most wholesome precept: 'Those who endure to the end will be saved,'[30] and again, 'If you continue in my word, you are my disciples; and you will know the truth, and the truth will make you free.'[31] My dear brothers and sisters, we must endure and persevere so that having tasted the hope of truth and freedom, we may finally attain its reality. It is this dynamic that gives us Christians our faith and hope. But if that faith and hope are to be fulfilled, then we need to be patient. We are pursuing a future glory, not the glory of this present world. We should ponder the words of the apostle Paul: 'In hope we were saved. Now hope that is seen is not hope. For who hopes for what is seen? But if we hope for what we do not see, we wait for it with patience.'[32] Thus, waiting and patience are never wasted. They enable us to be formed more truly in what we have begun to be so that we may be ready to receive from God what we hope for and believe.

On Patience, 12-13.

Suffering and the victory of faith

There are certain people who are disturbed because this disease has attacked equally pagans and Christians. They talk as if being a Christian guaranteed the enjoyment of happiness in this world and immunity from contact with illness, rather than preparing us to endure adversity in the faith that our full happiness is reserved for the future. It disturbs some of our number that death has no favourites. And yet what is there in this world that is not common to us all? As long as we are subject to the same laws of generation we have a common flesh. As long as we are in this world, we share an identical physicality with the rest of humankind, even if our spiritual identity singles us out. Until this corruptible form is clothed with incorruptibility, and this mortal frame receives immortality, and the Spirit leads us to God the Father, we share with the rest of humanity the burden of our flesh.

When the soil is exhausted and the harvest poor, famine makes no distinction of persons. When an army invades and a city is taken, everyone suffers a common desolation. When the skies are cloudless and the rains fail, all alike suffer from the drought. When a ship goes aground on treacherous rocks, the shipwreck affects all who sail in her without exception. Diseases of the eye, attacks of fever, weakness in limbs, are all as common to Christians as to anyone else because this is the lot of all who bear human flesh in this world . . .

The righteous have always displayed a capacity for endurance. The apostles maintained such a discipline in obedience to the commandment of the Lord not to murmur in adversity, but to accept bravely and patiently whatever may happen to them in the world . . . [In the same way] the fear of God and faith in God ought to prepare you for anything. If you have lost all your worldly goods, or your limbs are racked by constant pain and discomfort, or you have lost your wife, your children or friends, and you are swamped by grief, do not let these things become stumbling blocks to your faith but rather battles. Such things should not undermine or break the faith of Christians but reveal their courage in the struggle. The pain which these current troubles can inflict on us is nothing when compared with the future blessings that are assured us.

There can be no victory without a battle: only when victory has been secured through engaging in the battle is the victor's crown bestowed. The true helmsman is recognised in the midst of a storm. The true soldier is proven on the battlefield. There can be no authentic testing where there is no danger. When the struggle is real, then the testing is real. The tree which has sent down deep roots is not disturbed by gales, and the ship that has been made of decent timber may be buffeted by the waves but will not be broken. When corn is beaten on the threshing-floor, the solid and heavy grains rebuke the wind, whereas the empty chaff is carried away on the breeze ...

To summarise: the difference between us and those who do not know God is that when misfortune comes, others complain and murmur, but we are not distracted by adversity from the true path of virtue and faith; indeed, in the midst of suffering we are made strong.

On the Mortality Rate, 8,11-13.

Christian unity

We ought to hold firmly and maintain our [Christian] unity, especially those of us who are bishops presiding in the Church, thereby revealing the episcopate to be one and undivided. Let no one deceive the Christian community through lies, or corrupt our faith in the truth by faithless treachery. The episcopate is one; it is a unity in which each bishop enjoys full possession.[33] The Church is likewise one, even though it is spread abroad far and wide, and grows as her children increase in number. Just as the sun has many rays, but the light is one; or as a tree with many branches finds its strength in its deep root; or as various streams issue from a spring, their multiplicity fed by the abundance of the water supply, so unity is preserved in the source itself. You cannot separate a ray from the sun any more than you can divide its light. Break a branch from a tree, and once broken it will bud no more. Dam a stream from its source, and the water will dry up. In the same way the Church, flooded with the light of the Lord, puts forth her rays throughout the world, but it is an identical light that is being diffused, and the unity of the body is not infringed. She extends her branches over the whole world. She pours out her generous rivers but there is one source, one Mother, abundant in the fruit of her own creativity. We are born in the womb of the Church; we are nourished by her milk; and we are animated by her Spirit.

The bride of Christ cannot commit adultery; she is pure and chaste. She knows but one home and guards the sanctity of its marriage-bed with chaste modesty. She keeps us for God and she directs the children she has borne into his kingdom. But whoever parts company with the Church and consorts with an adulteress, becomes estranged from the promises of Christ. Such a person is a stranger, profane, an enemy. No one can have God as Father who does not also have the Church as mother. If any were able to escape who were outside Noah's ark, then they might escape who are outside the doors of the Church.

But the Lord admonishes us and says, 'Whoever is not with me is against me, and whoever does not gather with me, scatters.'[34] Those who break the peace and concord of Christ are working against Christ. Those who are gathering elsewhere than in the Church, are scattering the Church of Christ. The Lord says, 'I and the Father are one.'[35] And again, it has been written concerning the Father, Son and Holy Spirit, 'and these three are one'.[36] Does anyone believe that this unity in the Church which depends on God's faithfulness, which is expressed in the heavenly sacraments, can be torn asunder and ripped apart by opposing wills? Whoever does not hold fast to this unity is not holding to the law of God, and therefore not holding to the faith of the Father and the Son, and has no hold upon life and salvation.

This sacrament of unity, this bond of enduring concord is exemplified in the Gospel when it says that [at his crucifixion] the tunic of the Lord Jesus Christ was not divided or torn. Instead, the entire garment was given away. Whole and entire, the garment became the possession of the one who cast the lot for his clothing. It is an image with which to understand thè reality of those 'who put on the Lord Jesus Christ'[37]. . . No one can claim to be a true Christian and possess the garment of Christ who tears and divides the Church of Christ.

On the Unity of the Church, 5-7.

NOTES

1   Robin Lane Fox, *Pagans and Christians*, Viking, London and New York, 1986, pp.273-6.
2   *To Donatus*, 2.
3   *Letters* 67.4.
4   Martyrdom was considered a gift of God and the Church discouraged people from provoking it. It was for this reason that Cyprian would flee from the civil authorities until he felt that his time for witness had come and that he was worthy. cf. *Letters* 81.
5   see *On the Lapsed*, and *Letters* 11 and 12.
6   *Letters* 73.21.
7   *On the Unity of the Church*, 6.
8   ibid. 5. Liturgically this idea received dramatic expression when the newly-baptised received not only their first communion, but also drank from a cup containing a mixture of milk and honey. The ceremony celebrated the Christian's entry into the promised land, a land 'flowing with milk and honey'. But it also reflected current medical practice because this was also a food given to infants shortly after their birth. Thus here was the Church caring for her new children in the same way that a mother would care for her baby.
9   Matthew 6: 6.
10   Jeremiah 22: 23-24.
11   Proverbs 15: 3.
12   Cyprian in fact says: 'First Book of Kings' following the Septuagint classification.
13   1 Samuel 1: 13.
14   Psalm 4: 4.
15   from the Letter of Jeremiah, sometimes listed as Baruch 6: 6.
16   John 1: 11-12.
17   1 Samuel 2: 30.
18   1 Corinthians 6: 20.
19   Leviticus 20: 7; 1 Peter 1: 16.
20   Matthew 25: 34.
21   Matthew 26: 39.
22   Luke 14: 33.
23   Matthew 6: 34.
24   1 Timothy 6: 7.
25   1 John 1: 8.
26   Matthew 7: 2.
27   Mark 11: 25.
28   Mark 14: 38.
29   John 17: 3.
30   Matthew 10: 22.
31   John 8: 31-32.
32   Romans 8: 24-25.
33   Cyprian's doctrine of collegial episcopal authority may have been suggested by the collegiate nature of magistracies under the Roman constitution. He is certainly using legal terminology here: 'Each bishop enjoys full possession (*in solidum*)'. There is a piece of common property. By holding a part of it individually, each owner has common possession of the whole. Thus all the bishops together – *in solidum* – sit on the 'chair of Peter'. Each bishop, therefore, to the extent of his

communion with the others, is the successor of Peter. The Bishop of Rome is the sign of the unity of the episcopate, but has no jurisdiction over his fellow-bishops. It is probable that Cyprian issued the treatise in two versions, one of which (giving a higher profile to the Bishop of Rome) being designed for circulation in Rome.

34 Matthew 12: 30.
35 John 10: 30.
36 1 John 5: 7.
37 Cyprian uses Christ's seamless robe (John 19: 23-24) as an image of Christian unity, and in his exposition weaves together language drawn from Paul (Romans 13: 14) and the Psalms: 'they clothe themselves with violence as a garment' (Psalm 73: 6).

SELECT BIBLIOGRAPHY

TEXTS and TRANSLATIONS
CCSL 3A, 111A.
CSEL 3 vols.
Letters edited in ET G.W. Clarke ACW (4 vols).
Born to New Life, edited and selected Oliver Davies, ET Tim Witherow, with introduction by Cyprian Smith, New City, London, Dublin, Edinburgh, 1991.
The Early Christian Fathers, selected, edited and ET Henry Bettenson, OUP, London, Oxford, New York, 1956, pp.263-273.

STUDIES
Hinchliff, Peter, *Cyprian of Carthage and the Unity of the Christian Church*, Chapman, London, 1974.

2

The Desert Tradition
VOICES IN THE WILDERNESS

'If you will, you can become all flame.'
ABBA JOSEPH

Deserts are not noticeably friendly places, let alone candidates for romanticisation. They are places of extremes: barren, beautiful, desolate, unpredictable, hostile, surprising, lonely, life-threatening. But in the paradox of grace, deserts have also been places of gift, of testing and of encounter with self, with the forces of evil, and with God.

In the Judaeo-Christian tradition the desert has acquired a unique significance. It was through the desert that Abraham and Sarah journeyed to Canaan in response to the call of God. It was in the wilderness that the people of Israel learned the lesson and privilege of dependence upon God in the vulnerability of trust. The great crisis in the life of Elijah involved a flight into the desert where, in a cave on Mount Horeb, God spoke to him not in earthquake, wind or fire, but in a 'still, small voice'.[1] The Judaean wilderness was the setting for the preaching of John the Baptist; and of course, following his baptism, Jesus himself was 'driven' into the wilderness by the Spirit to be tested. This matrix of imagery formed the theological backcloth for the emergence of Christian monasticism when, during the fourth century, thousands of men and women moved into the deserts of Egypt, Palestine and Syria.[2] Here, at the very margins of human society, Christians sought to give expression to their baptism in lives of austerity, solitude, penitence and prayer. They were seeking God, the coming of the kingdom, and their own salvation.

Of course, in the shadow of those who espouse lofty ideals are to be found others of more mixed motives. For example, it is clear that some

Christians fled to the desert to avoid persecution and simply stayed there. Some went to escape the burdens of high taxation or military service.[3] A variety of human motives behind the emergence of Christian monasticism must be acknowledged. Nevertheless, the primary impetus of the movement was an authentic response of ordinary men and women to the absolute claims of the Gospel.

'Why do the rich grind the faces of the poor?' Antony of Egypt is alleged to have asked.[4] Christians had regularly protested against corruption in civic life. With the cessation of persecution following the defeat of Licinius by Constantine in 323, certain Christians now also began to protest against laxity and compromise in the Church as a result of the mass influx of nominal converts. The flight to the desert, however, was more than a protest movement: Christians went to the desert to engage in spiritual warfare. It was as if the front line of battle had moved from the market place to the desert, and the arena of the conflict was the human heart. A new form of 'white martyrdom' was emerging in the Church, in which Christians witnessed to the sovereignty of Christ not by their blood, but by the totality of their discipleship. The words of Paul about spiritual warfare took on a heightened significance: the battle was no longer 'against flesh and blood' but 'against the spiritual hosts of wickedness in the heavenly places.'[5]

A brother asked an old man, 'How can I be saved?' The latter took off his habit, girded his loins and raised his hands to heaven, saying, 'So should the monk be: denuded of all the things in this world, and crucified. In the contest the athlete fights with his fists; in his thoughts the monk stands, his arms stretched out in the form of a cross to heaven, calling on God. The athlete stands naked when fighting in a contest; the monk stands naked and stripped of all things, anointed with oil and taught by his master how to fight. So God leads us to victory.'[6]

Three forms of monastic living gradually emerged. There were hermits who lived a solitary life; there were monks who lived in communities; and there were those who lived in small groups of three or four, usually as disciples of a spiritual elder. The essence of the spirituality of the desert was caught, not taught; and thus the role of the spiritual father or mother was vital. The *abba* or *amma* was someone who, knowing God in their own experience, could discern truly, and therefore help a brother or sister in his or her pilgrimage of faith. 'Some people,' Antony observed, 'have afflicted their bodies by asceticism, but they lack discernment, and so they are far from God.'[7] It is from the desert that the themes of discernment and spiritual direction enter Christian spirituality.[8]

Obedience, purity of heart, charity, radical simplicity of lifestyle, hospitality, and attending with the ear of the heart, were all hallmarks of a way of life that admitted no compromise. Monks were self-supporting, working with their hands. Their lives were entirely oriented to God. In this context, the life of Antony the Great (251-356) became a paradigm of the monastic vocation. Athanasius began to write an account of the saint's life within a year of his death. It achieved a wide circulation and proved highly influential in promoting the monastic ideal. Three extracts from it are included at the conclusion of this chapter. Antony's call was presented as a literal response to the words of Christ in the Gospel: 'If you would be perfect, go, sell what you possess and give to the poor, and you will have treasure in heaven; and come, follow me.'[9] The Greek word *teleios*, here translated as 'perfect', was understood in terms of wholeness, completeness, and personal integration. For the Christian, this meant walking in the way of the cross. It involved personal renunciation not for its own sake, but in order to follow Christ more truly. Christian monasticism was about discipleship, not about asceticism or the pursuit of moral perfectionism.

This fundamental insight may be further exemplified by the incident where friends sought out Antony after years of seclusion. According to Athanasius, they discovered him 'balanced, a man governed by reason'. The choice of language is significant: there is no rejection of the body as evil, Antony's perfection is viewed as a return to humanity's *natural* condition. Again, when Antony lived near an oasis deep in the interior, he cultivated the desert and lived at peace with the wild animals. The reader is being presented with a portrait of the recovery of Adam's condition before the fall, of paradise regained. In other words, here was a man fully alive.

Some letters of the Desert Fathers and Mothers have survived, but for the most part they were illiterate. Invariably, however, when they met, they would ask each other for a 'word', for some distilled wisdom of their experience of God. In due course these personal encounters, and the life-giving 'words' that emerged from them, were recorded by their disciples and circulated as biographies and anthologies. Space permits the inclusion of only a fragment of this material. In it we are given glimpses of our forebears as they were known to their contemporaries. We do not encounter gloomy, forbidding people, but men and women who were approachable and compassionate, and above all, people who had an understanding of sin and failure. A monk was asked what they did all day. He replied: 'We fall down and get up; we fall down and get up; we fall down and get up.'[10]

With the increasing attacks of the barbarian invaders, monastic life (at least at Scetis in Egypt) became unviable. Seeds from its flowering, however, quickly disseminated throughout the Church, notably via Cassian to Benedict, and so to the West. The desert began to take on the quality of a cherished ideal, a golden age (albeit a highly compressed one) of intense spiritual renewal in the Church. The Desert Fathers and Mothers may not have been theologically sophisticated but they were real; and in their lively simplicity and directness, a wisdom may be discovered which is invigorating and authentic for every generation.

Solitude

The desert is much better than inhabited places for one who is seeking the glory of God, and the mountains are indeed preferable to cities for anyone aware of the grace that is given him.

Consider the little things. The animals of the desert are not subject to the whip and the mountain goats are not victims of shearers. Look at the wild ass in the desert; no one rides on his back. Watch the roebuck in the wild; he does not lose his freedom. Look at the stags on the rocks; they do not have to bear the yoke. Think of the wild beasts; they do not have to have their food doled out to them . . .

If an eagle makes its nest in a house its eyes suffer from the smoke. If the wild ass and the roebuck come down into the plain they are haunted by fear. If a ravening beast comes near city walls it forfeits its skin. A stag that goes down to the valley loses its antlers . . . The splendour and the beauty of wild beasts vanish on the plains. The strongest lions are overpowered, tamed and put in cages. So look to the animals, O man of the hills, and keep away from the dwellings of humanity.

Ephraim of Syria, *Sermon on Monks*, 3; ET Olivier Clement, *The Roots of Christian Mysticism*, London, 1993, p.211.

A brother asked Abba Sisoes, 'Why did you leave Scetis, where you lived with Abba Or and come to live here?' The old man said, 'At the time that Scetis became crowded, I heard that Antony was dead and I got up and came here to the mountain. Finding the place peaceful I have settled here for a little while.' The brother said to him, 'How long have you been here?' The old man said to him, 'Seventy-two years.'

Benedicta Ward, *The Sayings of the Desert Fathers*: Sisoes 28, p.183.

A brother came to Scetis to visit Abba Moses and asked him for a word. The old man said, 'Go and sit in your cell, and your cell will teach you everything.'

Sayings: Moses 6, p.118.

A brother questioned an old man, saying, 'My thoughts wander and I am troubled by this.' The old man said to him, 'Remain sitting in your cell and your thoughts will come to rest. For truly, just as when the she-ass is tied up her colt runs here and there but always comes back to his mother wherever she is, so it is with the thoughts of those who for God's sake remain steadfast in their cell: even if they wander a little, they will always come back to them.'

Benedicta Ward, *The Wisdom of the Desert Fathers*: 66, p.22.

Syncletica said, 'There are many who live in the mountains but behave as if they were in the town, and they are wasting their time. It is possible to be a solitary in one's mind while living in a crowd, and it is possible for one who is a solitary to live in the crowd of his own thoughts.'

Sayings: Syncletica 19, p.196.

Abba Lucius once said to Abba Longinus, 'If you have not first of all lived rightly with men, you will not be able to live rightly in solitude.'

Sayings: Longinus 1, p.103.

Silence

Abba Joseph said to Abba Nistheros, 'What should I do about my tongue, for I cannot control it?' The old man said to him, 'When you speak, do you find peace?' He replied 'No.' The old man said, 'If you do not find peace, why do you speak? Be silent and when a conversation takes place, it is better to listen than to speak.'

Benedicta Ward, *The Sayings of the Desert Fathers*: Nistheros 3, p.130.

Abba Poemen said, 'A man may seem to be silent, but if his heart is condemning others, he is babbling ceaselessly. But there may be another who talks from morning till night and yet is truly silent; that is, he says nothing that is not profitable.'

Sayings: Poemen 27, p.143.

A brother questioned [Abba Poemen] in these words: 'What does the Scripture mean "See that none of you repays evil for evil"?'[11] The old man said to him, 'Passions work in four stages: first the heart; secondly, in the face; thirdly, they are evident in words; and fourthly, it is essential not to render evil for evil in deeds. If you can purify your heart, passion will not come into your expression; but if it comes into your face, take care not to speak; but if you do speak, cut the conversation short in case you render evil for evil.'

Sayings: Poemen 34, p.144.

Abba Poemen said to Abba Amoun, 'If you can't be silent, you had better talk about the sayings of the Fathers than about the Scriptures; it is not so dangerous.'

Sayings: Amoun of Nitria 2, p.27.

44

Seeking God

An old man was asked, 'How can I find God?' He replied, 'In fasting, in watching,[12] in labours, in devotion, and above all, in discernment. I tell you, many people have injured their bodies without discernment and have gone away from us having achieved nothing. Our mouths smell bad through fasting, we know the Scriptures by heart, we can recite all the Psalms of David, but we do not have that which God seeks: charity and humility.'

Benedicta Ward, *The Wisdom of the Desert Fathers*: 90, p.29.

Abba Antony said, 'Our life and our death is our neighbour. If we gain our brother, we have gained God; but if we scandalise our brother, we have sinned against Christ.'

Sayings: Antony 9, p.2.

Abba Nilus said, 'Do not be always wanting everything to turn out as you think it should, but rather as God pleases; then you will be undisturbed and thankful in your prayer.'

Sayings: Nilus 7, p.129.

An old man said, 'The reason why we do not make progress is because we do not know our own measure, and we do not persevere in the work we undertake, and we want to acquire virtue without labour.'

Wisdom: 164, p.47.

Abba Poemen said, 'Vigilance, self-knowledge and discernment; these are the guides of the soul.' He also said, 'To throw yourself before God, not to measure your progress, to leave behind all self-will; these are the instruments for the work of the soul.'

Sayings: Poemen 35 and 36, p.145.

Differing ways to God

It was told of a brother who came to see Abba Arsenius at Scetis that, when he came to the church, he asked the clergy if he could visit Abba Arsenius. They said to him, 'Brother, have a little refreshment and then go and see him.' 'I shall not eat anything,' he said, 'till I have met him.' So, because Arsenius' cell was far away, they sent a brother with him.

Having knocked on the door, they entered, greeted the old man and sat down without saying anything. Then the brother from the church said 'I will leave you. Pray for me.' Now the visiting brother, not feeling at ease with the old man, said 'Wait. I will come with you,' and they went away together.

Then the visitor asked 'Take me to Abba Moses, who used to be a robber.' When they arrived the Abba welcomed them joyfully and then took leave of them with delight. The brother who had brought the other one said to his companion, 'See, I have taken you to the foreigner and to the Egyptian; which of the two do you prefer?' 'As for me,' he replied, 'I prefer the Egyptian.'

Now a Father who heard this prayed to God saying, 'Lord, explain this matter to me: for your name's sake the one flees from men, and the other, for your name's sake, receives them with open arms.' Then two large boats were shown to him on a river and he saw Abba Arsenius and the Spirit of God sailing in the one, in perfect peace; and in the other was Abba Moses with the angels of God, and they were all eating honey cakes.

Benedicta Ward, *The Sayings of the Desert Fathers*: Arsenius 38, p.15.

Obedience

One of the old men said, 'When Saint Basil came to the monastery one day, he said to the abbot, after the customary exhortation, "Have you a brother here who is obedient?" The other replied, "They are all your servants, master, and strive for their salvation." But he repeated, "Have you a brother who is really obedient?" Then the abbot led a brother to him and Saint Basil used him to serve during the meal. When the meal was ended, the brother brought him some water for rinsing his hands and Saint Basil said to him, "Come here, so that I also may offer you water." The brother allowed the bishop to pour the water. Then Saint Basil said to him, "When I enter the sanctuary, come, that I may ordain you deacon." When this was done, he ordained him priest and took him with him to the bishop's palace because of his obedience.'

Benedicta Ward, *The Sayings of the Desert Fathers*: Basil the Great 1, p.33.

It was said of Abba John the Dwarf that he withdrew and lived in the desert at Scetis with an old man of Thebes. His abba, taking a piece of dry wood, planted it and said to him, 'Water it every day with a bottle of water, until it bears fruit.' Now the water supply was so far away that he had to leave in the evening and return the following morning. At the end of three years the wood came to life and bore fruit. Then the old man took some of the fruit and carried it to the church and said to the brethren, 'Take and eat the fruit of obedience.'

Sayings: John the Dwarf 1, p.73.

An old man said, 'If someone, with the fear of God and in humility, orders a brother to do something, his word, uttered for the sake of God, causes the brother to submit and fulfil what was ordered. But if someone wishes to command a brother, not according to the fear of God but to subject him to his own authoritarian power, God, who sees the secrets of the heart, will not move the brother to listen and to fulfil it. The work which is done for God's sake is evident; that which is done through authoritarianism is also evident. The work of God is humble and it cheers; that which proceeds from authoritarianism is full of agitation and trouble, for it proceeds from evil.'

Wisdom: 183, p.50.

An old man said, 'The prophets wrote books, then came our Fathers who put them into practice. Those who came after them learnt them by heart. Then came this present generation, who have written them out and put them into their window seats without using them.'

Wisdom, 96, p.31.

Forgiveness

A brother at Scetis committed a fault. A council was called to which Abba Moses was invited, but he refused to go. Then the priest sent someone to say to him, 'Come, for everyone is waiting for you.' So he got up and went. He took a leaking jug, filled it with water and carried it with him. The others came out to meet him and said to him, 'What is this, Father?' The old man said to them, 'My sins run out behind me, and I do not see them, and today I am coming to judge the errors of another.' When they heard this they said no more to the brother but forgave him.

Benedicta Ward, *The Sayings of the Desert Fathers*: Moses 2, p.117.

A brother who had sinned was turned out of the church by the priest. Abba Bessarion got up and went with him, saying, 'I, too, am a sinner.'

Sayings: Bessarion 7, p.35.

An old man used to tell how one day someone committed a serious sin. Filled with compunction,[13] he went to confess it to an old man; but he did not say what he had done, simply, 'If a thought of this kind comes upon someone, can he be saved?' And the old man, who was without the experience of discernment, said to him: 'He has lost his soul'. When he heard this, the brother said to himself, 'If I am lost, I may as well return to the world.' As he was returning, he decided to go and manifest his thoughts to Abba Sylvain. Now this Abba Sylvain possessed great spiritual discernment. Coming up to him, the brother did not say what he had done, but proceeded in the same way, 'If thoughts of this kind come upon someone, can he be saved?' The father opened his mouth and beginning with the Scriptures, he attempted to show him that condemnation is not the lot of those who have these thoughts. When he heard this, the brother's hope revived and he also told him what he had done. Like a good doctor, the father, with the help of the Scriptures, tended his soul, showing him that repentance is possible for those who seriously turn to God. Later on, our abba went to visit the other father, and related all this to him, and said, 'Look how he who despaired of himself and was on the point of returning to the world, has become a star in the midst of his brethren.' I have related this so that we may know what danger there is in manifestation, whether of thoughts or of sins, to those who do not have discernment.

Wisdom: 85, p.28.

The gift of discernment

Amma Theodora said that a teacher ought to be a stranger to the desire for domination, vain-glory, and pride; one should not be able to fool him by flattery, nor blind him by gifts, nor conquer him by the stomach, nor dominate him by anger; but he should be patient, gentle and humble as far as possible; he must be tested and without partisanship, full of concern, and a lover of souls.

Benedicta Ward, *The Sayings of the Desert Fathers*: Theodora 5, p.72.

It was said of Abba Arsenius that once when he was ill at Scetis, the priest came to take him to church and put him on a bed with a small pillow under his head. Now behold an old man who was coming to see him, saw him lying on a bed with a little pillow under his head and he was shocked and said, 'Is this really Abba Arsenius, this man lying down like this?'

Then the priest took him aside and said to him, 'In the village where you lived, what was your trade?' 'I was a shepherd,' he replied. 'And how did you live?' 'I had a very hard life.' Then the priest said, 'And how do you live in your cell now?' The other replied, 'I am more comfortable.' Then he said to him, 'Do you see this Abba Arsenius? When he was in the world he was the father of the emperor, surrounded by thousands of slaves with golden girdles, all wearing collars of gold and garments of silk. Beneath him were spread rich coverings. While you were in the world as a shepherd you did not enjoy even the comforts you now have, but he no longer enjoys the delicate life he led in the world. So you are comforted while he is afflicted.'

At these words the old man was filled with compunction and prostrated himself saying, 'Father, forgive me, for I have sinned. Truly the way this man follows is the way of truth, for it leads to humility, while mine leads to comfort.' So the old man withdrew, edified.

Sayings: Arsenius 36, p.14.

Know yourself and your limitations

A bba Sarmatas said, 'I prefer a sinful man who knows he has sinned and repents, to a man who has not sinned and considers himself righteous.'

Benedicta Ward, *The Sayings of the Desert Fathers*: Samartas 1, p.189.

O ne day when [Abba John] was sitting in front of the church, the brethren were consulting him about their thoughts. One of the old men who saw it became prey to jealousy and said to him, 'John, your vessel is full of poison.' Abba John said to him, 'That is very true, abba; and you have said that when you only see the outside, but if you were able to see the inside as well, what would you say then?'

Sayings: John the Dwarf 8, p.73.

A bba Olympios said this, 'One of the pagan priests came down from Scetis one day and came to my cell and slept there. Having reflected on the monks' way of life, he said to me, "Since you live like this, do you not receive any visions from your God?" I said to him "No." Then the priest said to me, "Yet when we make a sacrifice to our God, he hides nothing from us, but discloses his mysteries; and you, giving yourselves so much hardship, vigils, prayer and asceticism, say that you see nothing? Truly, if you see nothing, then it is because you have impure thoughts in your hearts, which separate you from your God, and for this reason his mysteries are not revealed to you." So I went to report the priest's words to the old men. They were filled with admiration and said that this was true. For impure thoughts separate God from man.'

Sayings: Olympios 1, p.135.

A hunter in the desert saw Abba Antony enjoying himself with the brethren and he was shocked. Wanting to show him that it is sometimes necessary to meet the needs of the brethren, the old man said to him, 'Put an arrow in your bow and shoot it.' So he did. The old man said, 'Shoot another,' and he did so. Then the old man said, 'Shoot yet again,' and the hunter replied, 'If I bend my bow so much I will break it.' Then the old man said to him, 'It is the same with the work of God. If we stretch the brethren beyond measure they will soon break. Sometimes it is necessary to come and meet their needs.' When he heard these words the hunter was pierced by compunction and, greatly edified by the old man, he went away. As for the brethren, they went home home strengthened.

Sayings: Antony 13, p.3.

Amma Theodora said, 'There was a monk, who, because of the great number of his temptations said, "I will go away from here." As he was putting on his sandals, he saw another man who was also putting on his sandals and this man said to him, "Is it on account of me that you are going away? Because I will go before you, wherever you are going."'

Sayings: Theodora 7, p.72.

Some old men came to see Abba Poemen and said to him, 'When we see brothers who are dozing at the synaxis, shall we rouse them so that they will be watchful?' He said to them, 'For my part when I see a brother dozing, I put his head on my knees and let him rest.'

Sayings: Poemen 92, p.151.

Humility

An old man was asked, 'What is humility?' He replied, 'It is when your brother sins against you and you forgive him before he comes to ask you for forgiveness.'

Benedicta Ward, *The Wisdom of the Desert Fathers*: 171, p.48.

Once an anchorite[14] said to a brother, 'Please will you be so kind as to take me to see Abba Poemen?' So the brother brought him to the old man and presented him, saying, 'This is a great man, full of charity, who is held in high estimation in his district. I have spoken to him about you, and he has come because he wants to see you.' So Abba Poemen received him with joy. They greeted one another and sat down. The visitor then began to speak of the Scriptures, of spiritual and heavenly things. But Abba Poemen turned his face away and answered nothing. Seeing that he would not speak to him, the other brother went away deeply grieved and said to the brother who had brought him, 'I have made this long journey in vain. I have come to see the old man and he does not wish to speak to me.' Then the brother went inside to Abba Poemen and said to him, 'Abba, this great man who has so great a reputation in his own country has come here because of you. Why did you not speak to him?' The old man said, 'He is great and speaks of heavenly things and I am lowly and speak of earthly things. Now if he had spoken of the passions of the soul, I should have replied, but he speaks of spiritual things and I know nothing about that.' Then the brother came out and said to the visitor, 'The old man does not readily speak of the Scriptures, but if anyone consults him about the passions of the soul, he replies.' Filled with compunction, the visitor returned to the old man and said to him, 'What should I do, Abba, for the passions of the soul master me?' The old man turned towards him and replied joyfully, 'This time, you come as you should. Now open your mouth concerning this and I will fill it with good things.' Greatly edified, the other said to him, 'Truly, this is the right way!' And he returned to his own country giving thanks to God that he had been counted worthy to meet so great a saint.

Benedicta Ward, *The Sayings of the Desert Fathers*: Poemen 8, p.140.

One day some old men came to see Abba Antony. In the midst of them was Abba Joseph. Wanting to test them, the old man suggested a text from the Scriptures, and beginning with the youngest, he asked them what it meant. Each gave his opinion as he was able. But to each one the old man said, 'You have not understood it.' Last of all he said to Abba Joseph, 'How would you explain this saying?' and he replied 'I do not know.' Then Abba Antony said, 'Indeed, Abba Joseph has found the way, for he has said: "I do not know."'

Sayings: Antony 17, p.3.

A bba Marcarius was asked, 'How should one pray?' The old man said, 'There is no need at all to make long discources; it is enough to stretch out one's hand and say "Lord, as you will, and as you know, have mercy." And if the conflict grows fiercer say, "Lord, help!" God knows very well what we need and he shews us his mercy.'

Sayings: Macarius 19, p.111.

A bba Poemen said, 'As the breath which comes out of our nostrils, so do we need humility and the fear of God.'

Sayings: Peomen 49, p.146.

Love

Going to town one day to sell some small articles, Abba Agathon met a cripple on the roadside, paralysed in both legs, who asked him where he was going. Abba Agathon replied, 'To town in order to sell some things.' The other said, 'Do me a favour of carrying me there.' So he carried him to the town. The cripple said to him, 'Put me down where you sell your wares.' He did so. When he had sold an article, the cripple asked, 'What did you sell it for?' and he told him the price. The other said, 'Buy me a cake,' and he bought it. When Abba Agathon had sold a second article, the sick man asked, 'How much did you sell it for?' And he told him the price of it. Then the other said, 'Buy me this,' and he bought it. When Agathon, having sold all his wares, wanted to go, he said to him, 'Are you going back?' and he replied 'Yes.' Then said he, 'Do me the favour of carrying me back to the place where you found me.' Once more picking him up, he carried him back to that place. Then the cripple said, 'Agathon, you are filled with divine blessings, in heaven and on earth.' Raising his eyes, Agathon saw no one; it was an angel of the Lord, come to try him.

Benedicta Ward, *The Sayings of the Desert Fathers*: Agathon 30, p.21.

Abba Agathon said, 'If I could meet a leper, give him my body and take his, I should be very happy.' That indeed is perfect charity.

Sayings: Agathon 26, p.20.

Abba Antony said, 'I no longer fear God, but I love him. For love casts out fear.'

Sayings: Antony 32, p.6.

Work

A bba Moses said, 'If a man's deeds are not in harmony with his prayer, he labours in vain.'

Benedicta Ward, *The Sayings of the Desert Fathers*: Moses 4, p.120.

S ome monks who are called 'Euchites'[15] went to Enaton to see Abba Lucius. The old man asked them, 'What is your manual work?' They said, 'We do not touch manual work but as the Apostle says, we pray without ceasing.'[16] The old man asked them if they did not eat and they replied they did. So he said to them, 'When you are eating, who prays for you then?' Again he asked them if they did not sleep and they replied they did. And he said to them, 'When you are asleep, who prays for you then?' They could not find any answer to give him. He said to them, 'Forgive me, but you do not act as you speak. I will show you how, while doing my manual work,[17] I pray without interruption. I sit down with God, soaking my reeds and plaiting my ropes, and I say, "God, have mercy on me; according to your great goodness and according to your many mercies, save me from my sins."' So he asked them if this were not prayer and they replied that it was. Then he said to them, 'So when I have spent the whole day working and praying, making thirteen pieces of money more or less, I put two pieces outside the door and I pay for my food with the rest of the money. Whoever takes the two pieces of money prays for me when I am eating and when I am sleeping; so, by the grace of God, I fulfil the precept to pray without ceasing.'

Sayings: Lucius 1, p.102.

I t is said of Abba Pambo that as he was dying, at the very hour of his death, he said to the holy men who were standing near him, 'Since I came to this place of the desert and built my cell and dwelt here, I do not remember having eaten bread which was not the fruit of my hands and I have not uttered a word that I have lived to regret up to the present time; and yet I am going to God as one who has not yet begun to serve him.'

Sayings: Pambo 8, p.165.

Prayer

Prayer is a conversation of the spirit with God.

Evagrius of Pontus, *On Prayer*, 3; Philokalia I, 177.

The brethren asked Abba Agathon, 'Amongst all good works, which is the virtue which requires the greatest effort?' He answered, 'Forgive me, but I think there is no labour greater than that of prayer to God. For every time a man wants to pray, his enemies, the demons, want to prevent him, for they know that it is only by turning him from prayer that they can hinder his journey. Whatever good work a man undertakes, if he perseveres in it, he will attain rest. But prayer is warfare to the last breath.'

Benedicta Ward, *The Sayings of the Desert Fathers*: Agathon 9, p.18.

It is related of Amma Sarah that for thirteen years she waged warfare against the demon of fornication. She never prayed that the warfare should cease but she said, 'O God, give me strength.'

Sayings: Sarah 1, p.192.

Prayer changes at every moment in proportion to the degree of purity in the soul and in accordance with the extent to which the soul is moved either by outside influence or of itself. Certainly the same kind of prayers cannot be uttered continuously by any one person. A lively person prays in one way. A person brought down by the weight of gloom or despair prays in another. One prays in a certain way when the life of the spirit is flourishing, and in another way when pushed down by the mass of temptation. One prays differently, depending on whether one is seeking the gift of some grace or virtue or the removal of some sinful vice. The prayer is different once again when one is sorrowing at the thought of hell and the fear of future judgement, or when one is fired by hope and longing for future blessedness, when one is in need or peril, in peace or tranquillity, when one is flooded with the light of heavenly mysteries or when one is hemmed in by aridity in virtue and staleness in one's thinking.

John Cassian, *Conferences* IX, 8; ET Colm Luibheid, p.107.

The various kinds of prayer [petition, promise, intercession, pure praise] are followed by a higher state still...it is the contemplation of God alone, an immeasurable fire of love. The soul settles in it and sinks into its depths.

57

It converses with God as with its own Father, very familiarly, with special tenderness. That we have a duty to aim for this state, we are taught by the very text of the Lord's Prayer, since it says, 'Our Father'. We thereby profess that the God and Lord of the universe is our Father, and thereby profess the certainty that we have been called from the condition of slaves to that of adopted children.[18] . . . The prayer 'Our Father' raises those who make themselves familiar with it to that prayer of fire which very few know from experience. It is an ineffable state that is far above all human feeling, without the sound of any voice, without any movement of the tongue, without any articulate word. The soul is wholly filled with light and no longer makes use of human language, which is always limited. But it engrosses the whole person and becomes an abundant spring from which prayer flows and soars in an ineffable fashion up to God. It says so many things in this brief space of time that it cannot easily express them or even remember them when it returns to itself.

John Cassian, *Conferences* IX, 18, 25; ET Olivier Clement, *The Roots of Christian Mysticism*, New City, London, Dublin, Edinburgh, 1993, p.207.

The excellence of prayer does not consist in its quantity but in its quality.

Evagrius of Pontus, *On Prayer*, 151; Philokalia I, 189.

An invitation to glory

Abba Paul said: 'Keep close to Jesus.'

Benedicta Ward, *The Sayings of the Desert Fathers*: Paul the Great 4, p.172.

Abba Antony said, 'A time is coming when men will go mad, and when they see someone who is not mad, they will attack him saying, "You are mad, you are not like us."'

Sayings: Antony 25, p.5.

Abba Joseph said to Abba Lot: 'You cannot be a monk unless you become like a consuming fire.'

Sayings: Joseph 6, p.88.

Abba Bessarion, at the point of death, said, 'The monk ought to be as the Cherubim and Seraphim: all eye.'

Sayings: Bessarion 11, p.35.

The devil appeared to a brother disguised as an angel of light and said to him, 'I am Gabriel and I have been sent to you.' The brother said to him, 'See if it is not someone else to whom you have been sent; as for me, I am not worthy of it' – and immediately the devil vanished.

Benedicta Ward, *The Wisdom of the Desert Fathers*: 178, p.50.

Abba Poemen said concerning Abba Prior that every day he made a new beginning.

Sayings: Peomen 85, p.150.

Abba Lot went to see Abba Joseph and said to him, 'Abba, as far as I can, I say my little office, I fast a little, I pray and meditate, I live in peace and as far as I can, I purify my thoughts. What else can I do?' Then the old man stood up and stretched his hands towards heaven. And his fingers became like ten lamps of fire and he said to him, 'If you will, you can become all flame.'

Sayings: Joseph 7, p.88.

The call of Antony

Antony was an Egyptian by race. His parents were well born and prosperous, and since they were Christians, he also was reared in a Christian manner ... [Following their death] he was left alone with one quite young sister. He was about eighteen or even twenty years old, and he was responsible both for the home and his sister. Six months had not passed since the death of his parents when, going to the Lord's house as usual and gathering his thoughts, he considered while he walked how the apostles, forsaking everything, followed their Saviour, and how in the Acts [of the Apostles] some sold what they possessed and took the proceeds and placed them at the feet of the apostles for distribution among those in need, and what great hope is stored up for such people in heaven.

He went into the church pondering these things, and just then it happened that the Gospel was being read, and he heard the Lord saying to the rich young man: 'If you would be perfect, go sell what you possess and give to the poor, and you will have treasure in heaven.'[19] It was as if by God's design he held the saints in his recollection, and as if the passage were read on his account. Immediately Antony went out from the Lord's house and gave to the townspeople the possessions he had from his forebears (three hundred and very beautiful *arourae*[20]), so that they would not disturb him or his sister in the least. And selling all the rest that was portable, when he had collected sufficient money, he donated it to the poor, keeping back a few things for his sister.

But when, entering the Lord's house once more, he heard in the Gospel the Lord saying: 'Do not be anxious about tomorrow',[21] he could not remain any longer, but going out he gave those remaining possessions also to the needy. Placing his sister in the charge of respected and trusted virgins, and giving her over to the convent for rearing, he devoted himself from then on to the discipline rather than to the household, giving heed to himself and patiently training himself. There were not yet many monasteries in Egypt, and no monk knew at all the great desert, but each of those wishing to give attention to his life disciplined himself in isolation, not far from his own village ... At first Antony also began by remaining in places proximate to his village. And going forth from there, if he heard of some zealous person anywhere, he searched him out like the wise bee ...

He worked with his hands, having heard that he who is idle, 'let him not eat.'[22] He spent what he made partly on bread, and partly on those in need. He prayed constantly, since he learned also that it is necessary to pray unceasingly in private.[23] For he paid such close attention to what was read that nothing from Scripture did he fail to take in – rather he grasped everything, and in him the memory took the place of books. Living his life in this way, Antony was loved by all. He was sincerely obedient to those men of zeal he visited, and he considered carefully the advantage in zeal and in ascetic living that each held in relation to him. He observed the graciousness of one, the eagerness for prayers in another, he took careful note of one man's freedom from anger, and the human concern of another. And he paid attention to one while he lived a watchful life, or one who pursued studies, as also he admired one for patience, and another for fastings and sleeping on the ground. The gentleness of one and the long-suffering of yet another he watched closely. He marked, likewise, the piety toward Christ and the mutual love of them all. And having been filled in this manner, he returned to his own place of discipline, from that time gathering the attributes of each in himself, and striving to manifest in himself what was best from all ... Seeing him living thus, people used to call him 'God-loved', and some hailed him as 'son', and some as 'brother'.

Athanasius, *The Life of Antony*, 1-4; ET Robert Gregg, pp.30-3.

Antony in the desert

Antony spent nearly twenty years in this manner pursuing the ascetic life by himself, not venturing out and only occasionally being seen by anyone. After this, when many possessed the desire and will to emulate his asceticism, some of his friends came and tore down and forcefully removed the door [to the deserted fort where he was living]. Antony came forth as if from some shrine, having been led into divine mysteries and inspired by God...When they beheld him, they were amazed to see that his body had maintained its former condition, neither fat from lack of exercise, nor emaciated from fasting and combat with demons, but was just as they had known him before his withdrawal. The state of his soul was one of purity, for it was not constricted by grief, nor relaxed by pleasure, nor affected by either laughter or dejection. Moreover, when he saw the crowd, he was not annoyed any more than he was elated at being embraced by so many people. He maintained utter equilibrium, like one guided by reason and steadfast in that which accords with nature.

Through Antony the Lord healed many of those present who suffered from bodily ailments; others he purged of demons, and to Antony, he gave grace in speech. Thus he consoled many who mourned, and others hostile to each other he reconciled in friendship; urging everyone to prefer nothing in the world above the love of Christ. And when he spoke and urged them to keep in mind the future goods and the affection in which we are held by God, 'who did not spare his own Son, but gave him up for us all,'[24] he persuaded many to take up the solitary life. And so, from then on, there were monasteries in the mountains and the desert was made a city by monks, who left their own people and registered themselves for the citizenship in the heavens.

Athanasius, *op.cit.*, 14; ET Gregg, p.42.

Antony withdraws to the inner mountain

[Many people were besieging him, and increasingly Antony realised that it was not going to be possible for him] to retire as he intended and wished. He was apprehensive that because of the things the Lord was doing through him, either he would become proud or someone else might think more of him than was warranted. He considered things carefully and struck out, departing into the upper Thebaid, in the direction of people who did not know him. Receiving bread from the brothers, he sat down by the banks of the river, looking to see if a boat would come by . . . As if by the command of Providence, [some Saracen traders] eagerly welcomed him. After journeying three days and three nights in their company, he came to a very high hill. Below the hill there was water – perfectly clear, sweet and quite cold, and beyond there were plains, and a few untended date palms.

Then Antony, as if stirred by God, fell in love with the place . . . After first receiving loaves from his travelling companions, he remained on the mountain alone, no one else living with him. Looking on it as his own home, from that point forward he stayed in that place. Even the Saracens themselves, perceiving the zeal of Antony, would make it a point to travel that way and would joyfully bring loaves to him; but he also had a little modest relief from the date palms. In time, when the brothers learned of the place, they were anxious to send things to him, like children remembering a father. But Antony, seeing that some were burdened and suffered hardship on account of the bread, and being considerate for the monks in this matter, took counsel with himself and asked some of those who came to him to bring him a hoe, an axe, and a little grain. When he gathered these things, he inspected the land around the mountain, and finding a small, suitable place he ploughed it; and having abundant water from the spring, he planted it . . . [Later on, when people started coming to him yet again,] he also planted a few vegetables in order that the visitor might have a little relief from the rigour of that hard trip. At first, however, when the beasts in the wilderness came for water, they often would damage his crop and his planting. But gently capturing one of the beasts, he said to all of them, 'Why do you hurt me, when I do you no injury? Leave, and in the name of the Lord, do not come near here any longer.' From then on, as if being afraid of the command, they did not come near the place.

So Antony was alone in the inner mountain, devoting himself to prayers and the discipline. And the brothers who served him asked him if when they came every month, they might bring him olives and pulse and oil, for he was at this point an old man. Furthermore, we know from those who visited him, how many wrestlings he endured while dwelling there, 'not against flesh and blood,'[25] but against destructive demons. For there they heard tumults and many voices; and at night they saw the mountain filled with beasts. But they also observed Antony struggling as if against things visible, and praying against them; and he encouraged the ones who came to him, while at the same time he fought, kneeling and praying to the Lord. And it was truly amazing that being alone in such a desert, he was neither distracted by the demons who confronted him, nor was he frightened of their ferocity with so many four-legged beasts and reptiles there. But truly he was one who, as Scripture says, having 'trusted in the Lord' was 'like Mount Zion'[26], keeping his mind unshaken and unruffled; so instead the demons fled and the wild beasts, as it is written, made peace with him.[27]

Athanasius, *op.cit.*, 49-51; ET Gregg, pp.67-9.

NOTES

1   1 Kings 19: 12.
2   On the numbers of monks, see Ward, *The Lives of the Desert Fathers*, p.20.
3   The term 'anchorite' derives from the Greek verb *anachorein*, to withdraw or abandon. The anchorite was one who had withdrawn from society and retreated to the periphery of civilization in protest. In the Roman period the word had a specific application: it designated an individual who had fled from officialdom, repudiating all physical, military and financial obligations. In Coptic Egypt, the desert was the place beyond the reach of the tax collectors. In the Byzantine-Coptic literature of Christianised Egypt, the term as applied to Christian monks derived from this secular usage and highlights the element of protest in the origins of monasticism. See W.L.Westermann, 'On the Background of Coptism,' *Coptic Egypt*, New York, 1941, pp.12-13.
4   *Apophthegmata Patrum: The Alphabetical Collection*: Antony 2.
5   Ephesians 6: 12.
6   Ward, *The Wisdom of the Desert Fathers*, 11, p.3.
7   Ward, *The Sayings of the Desert Fathers*, Antony 8, p.2.
8   Discernment (*diakrisis* – 'a right judgement in all things') was a gift of God given in response to a life of disciplined prayer. The holy men and women of the desert were sought after for their wisdom. They were seen as charismatic figures, bearers of the spirit. The thoughts, doubts and sins of a disciple were exposed to the discernment of a spiritual elder as an integral part of the process of monastic formation. Although the product of long experience, the gift was not the prerogative of the aged, as Cassian warned:

> Abba Moses told me: It is good not to hide the thoughts but to
> disclose them to discreet and devout old men; but not to men
> who are old merely in years, for many have found final
> despair instead of comfort by confessing to men whom they saw
> to be aged, but who in fact were inexperienced.

(*Conferences*, II, 10; ET Owen Chadwick, *Western Asceticism*, p.60).
9   Matthew 19: 21.
10 Tito Colliander, *The Way of the Ascetics*, London, 1960; as quoted by Kallistos Ware, *The Orthodox Way*, Mowbrays, London, 1979, p.173.
11 1 Thessalonians 5: 15.
12 It was the custom of monks to pray at night for extended periods or vigils. The monk was one who 'watched' for the coming of the kingdom. Like the cherubim, the monk was to be 'all eye': watching and alert for the Lord. In literature the monks are often presented as the guardians of the world's peace, constantly keeping watch on the frontiers, armed by the Spirit against attacks of the demons. cf., Ward, *The Lives of the Desert Fathers*, p.12.
13 The phrase 'compunction [of heart]' occurs throughout monastic literature but it is difficult to render well in modern English. In origin compunction was a medical term designating attacks of acute pain. Gradually it came to be applied to pain of the spirit. It designated a pricking or uneasiness of conscience, a remorse born of penitence. It described a radical openness to God which made possible moments of profound disclosure when falsity was stripped away, and the human heart was pierced by a perception of the truth that would ultimately lead to freedom and salvation.
14 see above n.3.

15 literally, 'men of prayer'.

16 It was thought that Paul's admonition 'to pray without ceasing' (1 Thessalonians 5: 17) could be fulfilled by the observance of set hours of prayer. Various reasons were given by writers for praying at different times of the day or night. It was a pattern of prayer probably inherited from the synagogue and later modified by Christian practice. At first there seem to have been four such 'hours' or times of prayer (until two more were added in the fourth century), and it was understood that all Christians would observe these. The Desert Fathers and Mothers, who had to be self-supporting, were concerned to develop a more meditative pattern of prayer that could be sustained while working. Some monks, however, notably the Euchites, claimed that their commitment to prayer was so all-encompassing that they had no time to work. This is the background to this passage.

17 The dignity and spiritual importance of manual work was stressed in monasticism (cf. 2 Thessalonians 5: 17; and *RB* 48). The weaving of baskets and the plaiting of ropes or mats which required only mechanical movements were favoured because a monk could sit in his cell the whole day, make articles for subsequent sale, and recite the Psalter at the same time. Sometimes they used brief formulae, usually from the psalms, to sustain their prayer. Sometimes in a quite natural way, the invocation of the name of Jesus was combined with the rhythm of breathing. According to Athanasius, '[Antony] called his two companions and said to them, "Always breathe Christ".' (*The Life of Antony*, 91). The Jesus Prayer: 'Lord Jesus, Son of God, have mercy on me, a sinner' does not seem to have taken definitive shape before the thirteenth century.

18 The Desert Fathers taught that in a person's relationship with God, three phases are to be observed. By grace, one progresses from the status of 'slave' (when one prays to God out of fear); to that of 'hireling' (when one prays for a reward: perhaps a feeling of peace or serenity, or indeed for the reward of heaven itself); until finally one rejoices in the status of 'sons and daughters' (when one prays to God as 'Father' in a freedom born of love).

19 Matthew 19: 21.

20 approximately 207 acres.

21 Matthew 6: 34.

22 2 Thessalonians 3: 10.

23 combining ideas in 1 Thessalonians 5: 17 and Matthew 6: 7; see also above n.16.

24 Romans 8: 32.

25 Ephesians 6: 12.

26 Psalm 125: 1.

27 see Job 5: 23; cf. Mark 1: 13.

SELECT BIBLIOGRAPHY
TEXTS and TRANSLATIONS
Antony
Athanasius, *Vita Antonii, PG* 26, 838-976.

*Athanasius, *The Life of Antony*, ET with introduction, Robert Gregg, Paulist Press, New York, 1980.

The Letters of St Antony the Great, ET, Derwas Chitty, SLG Press, Oxford, 1975.
Pachomius
Pachomian Koinonia; vol. 1: *The Life of St Pachomius and his disciples*, ET with introduction, A. Veilleux, Cistercian Publications, Kalamazoo, Michigan, 1980.
John Cassian
PL 49-50.

Conferences, selected and ET, Colm Luibheid, Paulist Press, New York, 1985.

Western Asceticism, selected and ET, Owen Chadwick, LCC XII, SCM, London, 1958; pp.190-289.
Evagrius of Pontus
Evagrius, *Praktikos; Chapters on Prayer*, ET, J.E. Bamberger, Cistercian Publications, Spencer, Mass., 1970.

Palmer, G.E.H., Sherrard, P., Ware, K.T., *The Philokalia*, ed., and ET of Russian text, vol. I, Faber, London and Boston, 1979.
Desert Fathers and Mothers
Apophthegmata Patrum: The Alphabetical Collection, PG 65, 72-440.

Apophthegmata Patrum: The Anonymous Series, Greek text partially published by Nau, *Revue de l'Orient Chrétien* 12-14 (1907-9), 17-18 (1912-13).

Verba Seniorum, PL 73, 855-1022.

Western Asceticism, ET, Owen Chadwick, LCC XII, SCM, London, 1958; pp.13-189.

*The Wisdom of the Desert, selected and ET, Thomas Merton, Sheldon Press, London, 1960.

*The Wisdom of the Desert Fathers: The Anonymous Series, ET and introduction, Benedicta Ward, SLG Press, Oxford, 1975.

*The Sayings of the Desert Fathers: The Alphabetical Collection, ET, Benedicta Ward, Mowbrays, Oxford, 1975/83.

The Lives of the Desert Fathers, ET, Norman Russell; introduction, Benedicta Ward, Mowbrays, Oxford, 1980/88.

Harlots of the Desert: A Study of Repentance in early Monastic Sources, ET, Benedicta Ward, Mowbrays, Oxford, 1987.

STUDIES
Anson, P., *The Call of the Desert*, SPCK, London, 1964.

Burton-Christie, D.,*The Word in the Desert: Scripture and the Quest for Holiness in Early Christian Monasticism*, OUP, 1992.

Chadwick, Owen, *John Cassian*, 2nd ed., CUP, 1967.

Chitty, D.,*The Desert a City*, Blackwell, Oxford, 1966; St Vladimir's Seminary Press, New York, 1966/77.

Gould, Graham, *The Desert Fathers on Monastic Community*, Clarendon Press, Oxford, 1993.

* These volumes are recommended for those wishing to read further in this area.

3

Basil the Great
PRAYER AND THE
PURSUIT OF HOLINESS

*'Consider all that is and praise its Maker who produced
such benefits for your pleasure, and strive to make
yourself worthy of it. And if you turn to God, you will
understand our origin and our destiny.'*

CONCERNING PARADISE

Travellers to Turkey who have ventured off the tourist routes into the arid interior of Cappadocia may have encountered the extraordinary rock churches which are carved out of the volcanic tufa in the region. Once these churches and their associated dwellings, were peopled with Christian monks; today they are mostly ruined, their silence speaking of a past Christian civilization. Not infrequently a group of three figures recurs in the frescoes of the churches, their faces gazing down at you. They are the Cappadocian Fathers: Basil the Great, his younger brother Gregory of Nyssa, and their friend Gregory of Nazianzus. These three men between them exercised a profound influence upon the development of Christian theology and the spirituality of the Greek speaking Church; and in so doing, they laid the foundation of what was to become Byzantine Christianity.

The most famous of the three was Basil. He was born in 330 into a distinguished Christian family and educated at the rhetorical schools first in his native Caesarea, then in Constantinople, and finally in Athens where he befriended Gregory of Nazianzus. He was amazingly gifted, and at the age of twenty-six returned to Caesarea to embark upon a legal career. However, under the influence of his elder sister Macrina, he gave up his position, received baptism and began to devote more and more of his energy to exploring the Christian faith. He visited various monastic settlements in Syria, Mesopotamia and Egypt, and was deeply impressed by the integrity of their way of life. Eventually he decided to pursue a life of prayer and solitude himself, and in 358 retired to the family estate at Annesis on the river Iris in Pontus. Other young men also seeking an ascetic life soon joined him, among them his friend Gregory of Nazianzus. The two friends became enthusiastic admirers of the spirituality of Origen and edited an anthology of his writings known as the *Philokalia*. It was during this period that Basil also founded a number of other monastic communities and out of his experience of communal life, wrote the two sets of monastic Rules for which he is justly famous, known as *The Longer Rules* (or *Detailed Rules*) and *The Shorter Rules*. They promoted a return to the apostolic life of the first Christian community, with a common life founded on charity, and expressed in work, social service, prayer and regular meditation on Scripture. Today he is honoured as the real founder of Greek monasticism, much in the same way as Benedict has come to be revered as the patriarch of Western monasticism. Indeed, its very name – 'Basilian' monasticism – underscores its debt to Basil. Extracts from his *Rules* are included in the selection that follows. They are remarkable for their pastoral sensitivity and balance.

For Basil, the monk was the Christian *par excellence*. Like Antony of Egypt before him, he was haunted by Jesus' words: 'If you would be perfect . . . '[1] And perfection[2] for Basil lay in obedience to Christ's two great commandments: to love God and to love your neighbour as yourself. But how could you fulfil the divine precept to love your neighbour if you were a solitary? Hence Basil's great question: 'Whose feet do you wash?' The solitary had no one to correct his defects, and no one with whom to share his spiritual gifts to their mutual up-building. This was the theological *rationale* behind Basil's promotion of the communal (cenobitic) form of Christian monasticism in contrast to the more solitary (eremitical) ideal prominent in Egypt. For Basil, the common life of the monastery offered greater possibilities for the exercise of service and mutual love.[3]

By 359 Basil was already in deacon's orders, and some five years later he was persuaded to become a priest. Unlike the Egyptian monks with their predilection for solitude, Basil considered it completely natural with his social and intellectual background to be ordained. His outstanding gifts and flair for organisation made an ecclesiastical career inevitable, and in 370 he succeeded Eusebius as bishop of Caesarea and metropolitan of Cappadocia. As a bishop he became tireless in his defence of the poor who were suffering as a result of the heavy taxation and the endemic economic crisis which afflicted the Eastern empire. Near Caesarea he organised a complete city of social service run by monks. The people gave it the nickname 'Basiliad'. It contained a guesthouse, a hospital, a refuge for the poor and homeless, an orphanage, a hospice for the elderly, and schools. He reformed the liturgy. Nine years as a bishop were sufficient for this man to earn the title 'Great' in his own lifetime.

Theologically, Basil made a considerable impact because of his persistent opposition to Arianism. The controversy focused on the teaching of a presbyter in Alexandria called Arius who taught that the Son is not 'one in being with the Father' from eternity, but is rather his first creation. The heresy received imperial support; but Basil not only resisted it, he became the chief exponent in the East of the Catholic view that was eventually to triumph after his death at the Council of Constantinople in 381. His treatise *On the Holy Spirit*, from which two extracts are included in this anthology, was influential in establishing a trinitarian consensus. It heightened the consciousness of the Church concerning the distinctive role of the Spirit in the pattern of human salvation. For Basil, the life of each person and the corporate life of the Church needed to be penetrated by the Holy Spirit to transform them and to make them conform to the divine nature. This process of transfiguration occurred most powerfully as people participated in the liturgy. Indeed, Basil's spirituality was essentially eucharistic. He conceived of humanity's relationship to God as one of thanksgiving and praise. He viewed it as something natural, implanted in us by God at our creation. It could not be taught but rather emerged as a spontaneous response to the divine beauty and the divine goodness.

Basil suffered poor health for most of his life and died prematurely aged forty-nine in 379. But he left an inheritance of writings which has ensured his continuing influence upon the life and mind of the Church.

The journey inwards: a personal testimony

What I do, day and night, in this remote spot,[4] I am ashamed to write to you about. I have abandoned my career in the city because I am convinced that it will only make me further depressed. Within myself, I am still largely unresolved: I am like a traveller on the ocean who has never been on a voyage before and becomes ill and seasick. Such folk moan because the ship is large and has such an enormous swell, and yet the moment they transfer into a smaller boat or dinghy, they are tossed about even more and become violently ill. Wherever they go, they cannot escape from their nausea and depression. My internal state is something like this. I carry my own problems with me wherever I go and there is no escape. So in the end, I have got very little out of my solitude. What I ought to have done, what would have helped me to walk securely in the footsteps of Jesus who has led me on the path of salvation, would have been to have come here long ago. Has not our Lord said: 'If any would come after me, let them deny themselves, take up their cross and follow me'?[5]

We must strive for a quiet mind. The eye cannot appreciate an object set before it if it is perpetually restless, glancing here, there and everywhere. No more can our mind's eye apprehend the truth with any clarity if it is distracted by a thousand worldly concerns . . . For just as it is impossible to write upon a wax tablet without first having erased the marks on it, so it is impossible to receive the impress of divine doctrine without unlearning our inherited preconceptions and habitual prejudices. Solitude offers an excellent opportunity in this process because it calms our passions, and creates space for our reason to remove their influence . . . Let there be, therefore, places such as this, where we may pursue such spiritual training without interruption, nourishing our souls with thoughts of God. After all, what can be better on earth than to imitate the choirs of angels, to begin a day with prayer, honouring our Creator with hymns and songs? And as the day brightens, to pursue our daily tasks to the accompaniment of prayers, seasoning our labour with hymns as if they were salt? Such soothing melodies compose the mind and establish it in tranquillity.[6]

Tranquillity, as I have said, is indeed the first step in the process of our sanctification, for through it our conversation is purged of idle gossip; our eyes are enabled to concentrate without searching for beautiful bodies to ogle at; our ears are not forever assaulted by invasive noise or worse still, by superficial chatter or revelry. With our senses thus reorientated, our attention is no longer dissipated and our mind is thrown back upon itself, and is able to begin its ascent to the contemplation of God. And then, when the beauty of God shines about it, we lose all self-consciousness – even to the point of giving no thought to our preoccupation with food and clothes. We enjoy a holiday from the mundane and instead devote our entire energy to the acquisition of eternal goods. Our one concern is to flourish in self-control and courage, justice and wisdom, and all those other virtues in their various categories which guide the good person in the proper conduct of life.

The best guide for discovering the way to conduct our life is the thorough study of Scripture. Here are to be found not only instructions about appropriate conduct but also, in the stories of blessed people, vital images of godly living which invite our imitation. In whatever respect any of us may feel deficient, by devoting ourselves to this process, we discover as if from a pharmacy, medicine for our sickness . . . Prayer after such reading will leave us refreshed and our love for God invigorated. Ideally, such prayer should imprint upon our minds a clear idea of God, and with God established in our memory, we experience his indwelling. We become the temple of God when our continuous meditation is no longer fragmented by anxiety and our mind no longer assailed by unexpected emotions. Let us then flee from material things and cling to God. Let us repudiate all feelings that invite us to self-indulgence and instead give our energy to the pursuit of virtue.

Letters, 2.

Growing in the love of God

You cannot teach anyone to love God any more than you can teach someone to enjoy the light or to cherish life. No one taught us to love our parents or those who brought us up. Similarly, but with all the more reason, we did not learn to love God as a result of a course of instruction, but because in the very nature of every human being has been sown the seed of an ability to love. Those who are enrolled as pupils in the school of God's commandments[7] have welcomed this seed, and by the grace of God, are in the process of cultivating it with care, nurturing it with knowledge, and so fostering its growth to maturity . . .

You will realise that the virtue of love, in spite of being only a single quality, in fact embraces in its power all the commandments. The Lord says: 'If anyone loves me, he will keep my commandments.' And again he says: 'On the two [great] commandments hang everything in the Law and the prophets.'[8] . . . As regards these commandments given to us by God, let me first of all say this: we have also received from God the ability to keep them. In consequence, we cannot object that God is demanding something unusual of us; nor can we boast as if we have done something that was greater than the power that has been given us . . . God would not have given us the commandment to love him without also giving us the faculty to do so. The proof of this cannot be verified externally but it can be observed in our own experience. For example, it is natural to desire beautiful things (though we may differ in our perception of what is supremely beautiful); or again, without being taught, we have affection for those nearest and dearest to us; or to give a further example, we spontaneously show goodwill to our benefactors.

What can be more wonderful to contemplate than the beauty of God? Can you envisage anything more delightful than the grandeur of God? Can you conceive of a yearning of the soul as powerful and irresistible as that which God inspires in the soul that has been cleansed of all evil and cries out ardently: 'I am wounded with love'?[9] Beyond description and defying explanation are the flashes of divine beauty. Although we could compare its brightness to the light of the morning star, the moon or the sun, such comparisons fall short of its true glory and are as far from reality as the deep shadows of a moonless night compared with the glare of the noon-day sun. The beauty of God is invisible to the eyes of the body; only the soul and the mind can perceive it. Every time it illumines one of the saints it leaves them with a wound of intolerable yearning, an aching that is so strong that it cries: 'Alas, that I am still in this exile.'[10] 'When shall I come and appear before the presence of God?'[11] . . . They discover an insatiable thirst for the divine

73

beauty and pray that their contemplation of the sweetness of the Lord may be brought to the fulfilment of eternal life.

So then, we naturally aspire to what is beautiful and desire it. And what is beautiful is also good and lovable. God is good. Everyone, therefore, who is desiring the good is in fact desiring God.

The Longer Rules, 2,1.

The mystery of God and the inadequacy of human language

The nature and majesty of God cannot be defined in language or comprehended by human intellect. It cannot be explained or grasped in any one phrase or concept, but requires a variety of language. Inspired Scripture has instructed the pure in heart, but only with difficulty, and then 'as in a mirror, darkly.'[12] For to see God face to face and to have our knowledge perfected is promised for the age to come, and then, only to those who are deemed worthy of it. But now in this present life, even though we be a Peter or a Paul, and though we see truly and be not deceived or subject to fantasy, yet must we always remember that we are still seeing 'as in a mirror, darkly.' So let us cherish what insights we have in this life with joy, as we wait for the perfection of hereafter . . .

When we study Scripture we become increasingly aware of its witness to the partiality of our present knowledge and the incomprehensibility of the divine mystery. As a person progresses in this life so horizons expand, and the prospect of achieving a satisfactory understanding diminishes. We wait for that day when the partial shall be abolished and the wholeness of perfection established. No single title is sufficient to declare the glory of God, and there is great danger in fastening upon one phrase as if it were all-sufficient. For example, one person says 'God' but that does not necessarily connote Father; and in the title 'Father', the idea of Maker is absent. And where in these titles are the others found in Scripture: goodness, wisdom, power, and so forth? Again, if we apply the term 'Father' to God (in the strict sense in which we habitually use it), then are we not predicating of God passions, sexual impulses, ignorance, weakness, and various things? Similarly with the term 'Maker'; in human construct this involves time, the use of materials and various instruments and assistance. But these images are wholly inappropriate when applied to God, and as far as is humanly possible, they must be excluded from our thinking. For, as I have said, though every mind were to be united in investigating the mystery of God, though every tongue were united in its proclamation, yet no one would be found worthy of comprehending what is by definition, incomprehensible.

Concerning Faith, 3.

Responding to the generosity of God

It is impossible to find a vocabulary worthy enough to describe the gifts of God, for they are so many as to be innumerable, and so wonderful that the single gift [of creation] is itself sufficient to prompt the offering of our thanks to the Giver . . . I have no time to speak of the richness and diversity of God's gifts. We will have to pass over in silence the rising of the sun, the circuits of the moon, the variation in air temperature, the patterns of the seasons, the descent of the rain, the gushing of springs, the sea itself, the whole earth and its flora, the life of the oceans, the creatures of the air, the animals in their various species – in fact everything that exists for the service of our life. But the supreme benefit [of creation] we cannot pass over, even if we wished to. To be silent about that is absolutely impossible for anyone with intelligence and reason; and yet to speak of it worthily is also impossible.

God made human beings in his image and likeness;[13] he deemed us worthy of knowledge of himself, equipped us with reason beyond the capacity of other creatures, allowed us to revel in the unimaginable beauty of Paradise, and gave us dominion over creation. When we were deceived by the serpent and had fallen into sin, and through sin into death and all that follows in its wake, God did not abandon us. In the first place, God gave us a law to help us; he ordained angels to guard and care for us. He sent prophets to rebuke vice and to teach us virtue. He frustrated the impact of vice by dire warnings. He stirred up in us a zeal for goodness by his promises, and confronted us with examples of the end result of both virtue and vice in the lives of various individuals. To crown these and his other mercies, God was not estranged from the human race by our continuing disobedience. Indeed, in the goodness of our Master, we have never been neglected: our callous indifference towards our Benefactor for his gifts has never diminished his love for us. On the contrary, our Lord Jesus Christ recalled us from death and restored us to life.

In Christ the generosity of God is resplendent; for [as Scripture says]: 'being in the form of God, he did not cling to equality with God, but emptied himself, assuming the form of a servant.'[14] What is more, he assumed our frailty and bore our infirmities; he was wounded on our behalf that by his wounds we might be healed.[15] He set us free from the curse, having become a curse on our behalf himself, and underwent the most ignominious death that he might lead us to the life of glory. Not content with restoring us to life when we were dead, he has graced us with the dignity of divinity and prepared for us eternal mansions, the delight of which exceeds all that we can conceive.

'What then shall we render to the Lord for all his benefits to us?'[16] God is so good that he asks of us nothing. He is content merely with being loved in return for his gifts. When I consider this – and here let me speak very personally – I am overcome with an awe and fear lest through my carelessness or my preoccupation with trivia, I should fall from the love of God and become a reproach to Christ.

The Longer Rules, 2, 2-4.

Life in the Spirit

Is there anyone who, on hearing the titles of the Holy Spirit, does not experience a certain exaltation as their mind contemplates that supreme nature? For it is called the 'Spirit of God',[17] 'the Spirit of truth who proceeds from the Father',[18] the 'right Spirit',[19] the 'guiding Spirit'.[20] But the chief and distinctive title is simply 'Holy Spirit', which is appropriate for that which is without material body and cannot be divided.

Our Lord when teaching the [Samaritan] woman [at the well][21] who thought God to be merely an object of local worship, said that 'God is Spirit'; in other words that God is without material body and unable to be comprehended. If we consider this statement, it precludes any idea of a circumscribed nature, subject to change and chance, or anything resembling a creature. On the contrary, we are compelled to push the categories of our thinking to the limit, and to conceive of the Spirit in terms of an intelligent essence,[22] of infinite power, of unlimited greatness, traversing all times and ages.

The Spirit is generous in bestowing gifts; and in response, every creature turns to the Spirit to be made holy. Those who are concerned to live virtuously reach out to the Spirit, and by the breath of his inspiration, are enabled to travel toward their natural and proper end. The Spirit lacks nothing because he is the source of all perfection. The Spirit needs no restoration because he is himself the supplier of life. The Spirit requires no additions because from all eternity the Spirit is abundantly full, self-established, present everywhere, the source of holiness and the light of our understanding, offering illumination to every mind that is searching for truth.

Although the Spirit is by nature inaccessible, yet through the generosity [of God] we can receive him. The Spirit fills all creation with his power,[23] but this reality is only apprehended by those who are worthy. Moreover, not everyone shares in the Spirit to the same degree, but rather [as Scripture says], the Spirit distributes his energy 'according to a person's faith.'[24] Thus the Spirit is simple in essence but manifold in power. The Spirit is present to each individual in fullness, and in fullness is present everywhere. The Spirit is shared, but does suffer division. All share in the Spirit and yet the Spirit remains entire, like a sunbeam whose gentle light falls upon a person who enjoys it as though the sun shone for him alone, whereas in reality the sun is shining over land and sea and mingles with the air. In the same way, the Spirit is present to all those who are capable of receiving him as if given to each of them uniquely, and sends forth grace sufficient and great enough

78

for all, yet without loss to itself; and we profit by sharing in this, but according to our capacity, not according to the Spirit's power . . .

Through the Spirit's aid hearts are raised on high, the weak are led by the hand, and those who are reaching forward in life are led on to perfection. Shining on those whose hearts are purified and stainless, the Spirit makes them truly spiritual through the intimate union they have been granted. As when a ray of light touches a polished and shining surface, and the object becomes even more brilliant, so too souls that are enlightened by the Spirit become spiritual themselves and reflect their grace onto others. The grace of the Holy Spirit enables them to foresee the shape of the future, to penetrate mysteries, to discern the meaning of obscure realities, to receive spiritual blessings, to focus their minds on their heavenly citizenship, and to dance with the angels. Thus is their joy unending and their perseverance in God unfailing. Thus do they become like God, and most wonderful of all, thus do they themselves become divine.[25]

On the Holy Spirit, 9, 22-23.

Baptism and paradise regained

The Lord, the Dispenser of our life, has inaugurated a covenant of baptism which carries with it the figure of death and the figure of life. Water is symbolic of death and the Spirit signifies the seal of life. This relates to the problem which has been raised as to why water and Spirit are associated in baptism. The reason is that baptism has two purposes: on the one hand, to destroy the body of sin[26] and prevent us from bearing fruit in death; and on the other hand, to give us life in the Spirit with its fruit borne in holiness. The water is a symbol of death: it receives the body as if it were into a tomb. The Spirit bestows life-giving energy, recalling our souls from the death of sin to the vitality they once enjoyed. This is what is meant by being 'born again of water and the Spirit'.[27] Death itself is killed in the water and the Spirit restores us to life.

The great mystery of baptism is accomplished with three immersions,[28] and with three invocations. In this way the figure of death is represented and the baptised are enlightened by the handing on of divine knowledge. If there is any grace in the water it is not because of any inherent power the water may possess but because of the presence of the Spirit. For [as Scripture asserts] baptism is 'not the washing away of dirt but the appeal made to God from a clear conscience.'[29] This is why the Lord, in order to prepare us for the resurrection life, lays before us the way of the Gospel. We are to avoid anger, practise patience, be detached from the pursuit of pleasure and the love of money. In this way, by the exercise of our own free choice, we are anticipating the character of the coming age . . .

Through the Holy Spirit paradise is regained for us; we are able to ascend to the kingdom of heaven and our status as adopted children of God is restored whereby we have the confidence to call God our Father. We share in the grace of Christ and are called 'children of light' and 'sharers in the eternal glory'. To put it simply, we are filled with all the blessings not only of this age but of that which is to come. We can observe as in a mirror, as though already present, the grace of the good things which are in store for us in the future, the enjoyment of which we receive now through faith. If the pledge is of this order, how wonderful must be the perfection! If the first fruits are so rich, how great must be the consummation!

On the Holy Spirit, 15, 35-36.

Whose feet do you wash?

I believe that a life lived in community is more useful than one pursued in solitude. To begin with none of us is self-sufficient. In regard to material needs and the necessities of life, we need one another's help. The foot, for example, is quite capable of doing certain things by itself, but divorced from other limbs its owner would soon realise that its capabilities are not sufficient for survival and are no substitute for what is lacking. This is what happens in the solitary life: what we have is not put to good use and what we lack we cannot obtain. God our Creator has ordained that we need each other so that, as Scripture reminds us,[30] we are bonded together.

Quite apart from this, Christ's commandment to love does not permit us to be self-centred. Again, as Scripture asserts: 'Love does not seek its own interest.'[31] The solitary life, by contrast, has but one aim: the service of the needs of the individual. This is plainly in conflict with the law of love. Let it suffice to consider how the apostle [Paul] kept this law: 'I did not seek my own advantage, but that of many that they might be saved.'[32] Furthermore, it is difficult for solitaries to discover their faults simply because they have no one to point them out and no one to set them right with kindness and compassion. A reproof, even if it comes from an opponent, often induces a desire for improvement in a good person; and when it comes from someone who loves us tenderly, a skilful cure is effected. As Scripture says: 'When a person loves, correction is given with prudence.'[33] But it is difficult to find such a guide when you live in solitude, unless you have already established a link with someone having lived first in community . . .

Now all of us alike have received the one hope of our calling: we are united in one body with Christ as head, each of us serving severally as members one to another. If we are not joined together in harmony in the intimacy of one body in the Holy Spirit, but each of us is opting for solitude, refusing to contribute to the common life in a way which is pleasing to God, and instead gratifying our own selfish needs, then how can we preserve a genuine mutuality of service or know our common subjection to Christ as head? We cannot rejoice with those who rejoice or suffer alongside someone in pain if we live in isolation because it is impossible to be aware of the needs of our neighbour. Furthermore, no individual is the recipient of all spiritual gifts: spiritual gifts are distributed by the Spirit according to each person's faith. Consequently, in the common life the personal gift becomes the property of all. [As the apostle Paul says:] 'To one is given wisdom; to another knowledge; to another faith; to another gifts of healing, and so forth.'[34] Each of these gifts is granted as much for the sake of others as for the sake of the recipient. In the life of a community, the working of the Holy Spirit in one person diffuses into the life of all . . .

Again, how can you grow in humility if there is no one against whom you can compare yourself? How can you demonstrate compassion when you are cut off from communion with your fellows? How can anyone grow in patience when there is no one to frustrate your wishes? If any claim to find the teaching of Holy Scripture quite sufficient to correct their character without anybody else's help, they are making themselves out to be like an architect who knows the theory of construction but is unable to put theory into practice, or like a smith who prefers not to practise his trade. To such as these are the words of the apostle addressed: 'It is not the hearers of the Law who are righteous before God but the doers of the Law who shall be justified.'[35] Our Lord, in loving every human being right to the end, did not limit himself to teaching us in words. In order to give us a precise and clear example of humility in the perfection of love, he took a towel and washed his disciples' feet. So what about you, living entirely on your own, how will you ever discover such humility? Whose feet will you wash? Whom will you care for? How in your solitude will you discover 'how good and how lovely it is when brothers live together in unity'? – an experience which the Holy Spirit likens to the fragrant oil that flowed down from the High Priest's head.[36]

Living in community is like life in the arena: it is an inner journey, an experience of being continuously stretched as you strive to keep the commandments. Its sole object is to give glory to God according to the words of our Lord Jesus Christ: 'Let your light so shine before others that they may see your good works and give glory to your Father in heaven.' [37]

The Longer Rules, 7.

Attending to God

It is very important to recognise that we will never succeed in keeping any of the commandments, in loving God or our neighbour, if our minds are perpetually distracted. For it is impossible to gain any accurate knowledge, be it in art or science, if one is always flitting from one subject to the next. It is impossible to master something without being prepared to persevere to the end. Our activity must correspond with our aims since nothing in this life is achieved by inappropriate methods. You cannot become an expert smith if you persist in doing pottery; athletes' wreaths are not won by practising the flute! For each end a proper and necessary effort is required.

Thus, we must practise the art of being well-pleasing to God according to Christ's Gospel, by disengaging from mundane preoccupations and by fostering a determined attention of the mind . . . Anyone who truly wishes to follow God must be free from the fetters that attach us to this world. We need to make a complete break with our former way of life. For example, unless we avoid all obsession with the body and the concerns of this world, we will never succeed in pleasing God. Our minds must be trained to another pattern of thinking; for as the apostle Paul says: 'Our citizenship is in heaven.'[38] Indeed, the Lord has stated quite clearly, 'Unless you renounce everything you possess, you cannot be my disciple.' [39] Having done this, it is vital that we be vigilant to ensure that we never distance ourselves from God, or obscure our memory of his wonders with our distracted imagination. It is important to cherish a pure thought of God, consciously imprinting it upon our memory as if it were an indelible seal. In this way we grow in love for God: it stirs us to fulfil his commandments and in so doing, the love of God in us is nurtured in perpetuity.

The Longer Rules, 5.

NOTES

1   Matthew 19: 21.
2   See discussion of term on p.40
3   It may also be that Basil was drawing upon his knowledge of urban ascetic
    Christian households and the monastic households often attached to some
    bishops. These were becoming increasingly popular in the East at this time.
    Certainly it was Basil who introduced the innovation of urban monasteries. The
    desert was already becoming a distant ideal and in its place, a new zeal for
    disciplined service within society was emerging.
4   This letter was written to Gregory of Nazianzus in about 358, upon Basil's move
    to Pontus in Cappadocia.
5   Mark 8: 34.
6   The aim of the ascetic life for Basil was to 'establish the mind in tranquillity
    (*hesychia*)'. Negatively, this involved the avoidance of distraction. Positively, it
    included discipline and prayer. Through the practice of tranquillity the soul was
    purified and ascended to the contemplation of God. cf. Gregory the Great, p.198,
    n.11.
7   cf. Benedict's use of the image of 'school' – *RB*, Prologue; p.176, n.21.
8   Basil is referring to Jesus' summary of the law: to love God and neighbour –
    Matthew 22: 40.
9   Song of Songs 2: 5.
10 Psalm 120: 5.
11 Psalm 42: 2.
12 1 Corinthians 13: 12.
13 Genesis 1: 26. A number of phrases in this passage are to be found in the liturgical
    thanksgiving of St Basil; see below n.25.
14 Philippians 2: 6, 7.
15 Isaiah 53: 4, 5; 1 Peter 2: 24.
16 Psalm 116: 12.
17 Matthew 12: 28 etc.
18 John 15: 26.
19 Psalm 51: 10.
20 Psalm 51: 12.
21 John 4: 24.
22 The Greek word here is *ousia* which may be variously translated as 'being',
    'essence', or 'substance'. It is the fundamental theological category with which
    the Fathers describe God, and here Basil uses the term directly of the Holy
    Spirit. He was one of the first Fathers to articulate the divinity of the Holy Spirit.
    cf. *On the Holy Spirit*, 10, 24; *Letters* 8, 11; 159, 2.
23 Wisdom 1: 7.
24 Romans 12: 6.
25 The purpose of the incarnation was to establish full communion between God and
    humanity so that in Christ, humanity may find adoption and immortality, often
    called 'deification' (in Greek *theosis*). Union with God by grace was upheld as
    the destiny of humanity: not by emptying human nature, but by fulfilling it in the
    divine life, since only in God is human nature truly itself. The Fathers commonly
    distinguished between the terms 'image' and 'likeness': 'image' was intepreted
    in relation to reason and freedom, that which distinguishes human beings from
    the rest of the animal kingdom; 'likeness' was interpreted in relation to man's

calling to become like God, to be deified, to become God by grace. Many Biblical texts were expounded: notably, 2 Peter 1: 4. This language was taken up by Irenaeus but made famous by Athanasius in his statement: 'God was made human that we might be made God' (*On the Incarnation*, 54). Deification did not mean absorption into the Godhead: we remain the distinctive persons we are. Rather, our entire humanity, body and soul, is to be transfigured through the power of the Spirit into the likeness of the divine nature.

26 Romans 6: 6.
27 John 3: 5 etc.
28 A threefold immersion in honour of the Holy Trinity had become the universal practice of the Church.
29 1 Peter 3: 21.
30 1 Corinthians 12.
31 1 Corinthians 13: 5.
32 1 Corinthians 10: 33.
33 Proverbs 13: 24.
34 1 Corinthians 12: 8-10 – shortened.
35 Romans 2: 13.
36 Psalm 133: 2.
37 Matthew 5: 16.
38 Philippians 3: 20.
39 Luke 14: 33.

SELECT BIBLIOGRAPHY

TEXTS and TRANSLATIONS
PG 29-32.
On the Holy Spirit, SC 17.
Letters, critical ed. and ET by R. Deferrari, 4 vols, Loeb Classical Library, London and Cambridge, Mass., 1926-34.
On the Holy Spirit introduction and ET by David Anderson, St Vladimir's Seminary Press, New York, 1980.
On the Holy Spirit and *Letters*, ET by B. Jackson, NPNF 8; (rather dated translation).
The Ascetic Works of St Basil, ed. and ET by W.K.L.Clarke, SPCK, London; Macmillan, New York and Toronto, 1925; (includes *The Longer Rules* and *The Shorter Rules*).
Bettenson, H., *The Later Christian Fathers*, OUP, Oxford, London, New York, Toronto, 1970, pp.59-98; ET of selected writings.
Witherow, T., *Gateway to Paradise: Basil the Great*, ET of selected writings with good introduction, New City, London, Dublin and Edinburgh, 1991.

STUDIES
Fedwick, Paul J., ed. *Basil of Caesarea: Christian, Humanist, Ascetic*, 2 vols, Pontifical Institute of Medieval Studies, Toronto, 1981.
Lossky, V., (ET) *The Mystical Theology of the Eastern Church*, James Clarke, Cambridge, 1957/1973.

4

Gregory of Nyssa
IN THE SHADOW OF HIS GLORY

'This truly is the vision of God: never to be satisfied in our desire to see God; but always, by looking at what we can see, rekindle our desire to see yet more.'

THE LIFE OF MOSES

Gregory of Nyssa was born at Caesarea in around 330, the child of an aristocratic Christian family which numbered martyrs among its members. He was educated in rhetoric and philosophy in the schools of Cappadocia, but unlike his elder brother Basil, he was academically undistinguished. We do not know at what stage he received baptism, but it was certainly not in infancy since even Christian families delayed baptism till after the traumas of adolescence. Gregory was introduced to the spiritual life by his elder sister Macrina with whom he maintained close bonds of friendship throughout his life, and indeed wrote her biography.[1] It was she who, after the death of their father, converted the household into a sort of monastery on one of the family estates.

It would seem that Basil and his friend Gregory of Nazianzus tried to persuade Gregory to join them in their ascetic enterprise, but contrary to some opinion, there is no evidence that they ever succeeded.[2] Indeed, from the outset Gregory displayed independence of mind. Originally destined for the priesthood, he chose instead a career as a rhetorician, and married Theosebia, a woman of great culture and strong faith, and with whom he continued to live even after becoming a bishop.[3]

In 372 Basil (now Bishop of Caesarea) had his brother nominated as bishop of the neighbouring town of Nyssa. Unfortunately, Gregory, who was introspective and shy with little aptitude for administration, was quickly

86

undermined by the strong Arian faction in the diocese[4] which succeeded in having him deposed and exiled. In 378, however, on the death of the Emperor Valens who had supported Arianism, Gregory returned to Nyssa as the champion of Nicene orthodoxy. The following year an even more momentous event occurred: both Basil and Macrina died. Suddenly, out of their shadow, Gregory emerged not only as their spiritual heir, but also as a gifted man in his own right and arguably the most original of the Cappadocian Fathers.

Against Eunomius who claimed that reason can cope with all that is real and therefore, by deduction, even God, Gregory asserted the immensity of God, his essential unknowability.[5] This became a dominant theme in his writings. To say that God was unknowable, however, was not the same thing as to state that God was impersonal. Indeed, for Gregory the essence of God was always love, a love moreover that was expressed in the suffering of Christ on the cross. God reveals his love through the self-emptying of the Son.[6] In Jesus the presence of God is certain, but also mysteriously hidden. This vein of paradox runs throughout Gregory's spirituality.

The starting-point for Gregory was always Scripture. Like his brother he was fascinated by the works of Origen and followed him in his devotion to the three books of wisdom in the Bible: Proverbs, Ecclesiastes and the Song of Songs. They marked out for him the spiritual way, a way which involved ethical change and the transformation of moral conduct (Proverbs), detachment from the material world (Ecclesiastes), and the expansion of the soul into the realm of divine love (Song of Songs).[7] But whereas Origen had taught that this spiritual journey is an experience of increasing illumination, for Gregory it was an experience of darkness.

In his treatise *The Life of Moses* he presented the experience of Moses climbing Mount Sinai and entering into the dark cloud of God's presence as the pattern of man's encounter with the divine. The mountain, like the desert, became an image of abandonment. There one was stripped of all egocentric concerns and transported by the stark landscape into an emptiness which only God could fill. Gregory took over Origen's schema of the three stages of prayer and related them to three episodes in the life of Moses: the revelation at the Burning Bush, and the two ascents of Mount Sinai, first into the cloud, then later into the darkness where Moses asked to see God face to face. Moses moved from the revelation of light (*phos*), to the darkness of the cloud (*nephele*), to thick darkness (*gnophos*) 'where God dwells'.[8] According to Gregory, the soul's ascent to God involves this ascent into divine darkness. The fact that one cannot see in the dark became a powerful metaphor in Gregory's hands with which to communicate the sheer struggle and bewilderment of prayer. Prayer for Gregory was an endless longing for God, a reaching out in faith and trust for the unknowable.

Gregory was the first to give systematic expression to what came to be termed 'apophatic theology' or 'negative theology'.[9] He recognised the relativity of all language and the consequent need to balance theological affirmations with negative assertions. Human constructs, even cherished religious imagery, can distort as much as disclose the mystery which is God. In Gregory's own words: 'Every concept formed by the intellect in an attempt to comprehend and circumscribe the divine nature, will succeed only in fashioning an idol, not in making God known.'[10] With Gregory such statements represent something more than a philosophical exercise. They point to the reality of a personal encounter with God which was profound and beyond all discursive thought. Prayer in this tradition of Christian spirituality is a *via negativa*, a path of 'unknowing'; it turns the soul 'away from the image' (*apo-phasis*), emptying the mind of all efforts to comprehend the holy. It requires the surrendering of all control because it has to do with the One who is hidden and incomprehensible, who upsets human definitions and expectations. Prayer involves a leap into the darkness. For Gregory of Nyssa, God is met not as an object to be understood, but as a mystery to be loved. It is a spirituality of pure adoration.

The mystery of the unseen God

Now the divine nature, as it is in itself, according to its essence, transcends every act of comprehensive knowledge, and it cannot be approached or attained by our speculation. Men have never discovered a faculty to comprehend the incomprehensible; nor have we ever been able to devise an intellectual technique for grasping the inconceivable. For this reason the great Apostle calls God's ways 'unsearchable',[11] teaching us by this that the way that leads to the knowledge of the divine nature is inaccessible to our reason; and hence none of those who have lived before us has given us the slightest hint of comprehension suggesting that we might know that which in itself is above all knowledge.

Such then is God whose essence is above every nature, invisible, incomprehensible. Yet he can be seen and apprehended in another way, and the ways of this apprehension are numerous. For we can see him, who has 'made all things in wisdom',[12] by the process of inference through the wisdom that is reflected in the universe. It is just as in human works of art, where the mind can in a sense see the author of the ordered structure that is before it, inasmuch as he has left his artistry in his work. But notice that what we see here is not the substance of the craftsman, but merely the artistic skill that he has impressed in his work. So too, when we consider the order of creation, we form an image not of substance but of the wisdom of him who has done all things wisely. Again, when we consider the origin of human life, how God came to create man not out of any necessity but merely by the goodness of his free will, we say that we again contemplate God in this way, but it is his goodness and not his essence that is the object of our knowledge. So it is with all the things which raise the mind towards the supreme good; in all of these cases we may speak of a knowledge of God, since all of these sublime considerations bring God within our ken.

On the Beatitudes, sermon 6; ET Herbert Musurillo, *From Glory to Glory*, pp.98-9.

The paradox of the spiritual quest

When we look down from the sublime words of the Lord into the ineffable depths of his thoughts, we have an experience like that of someone gazing down from a high cliff into the immense sea below. On the coastline one can often see rocky cliffs where the seaward face has been sliced off sheer from top to bottom, with their tops projecting outwards forming a promontory overhanging the depths. If anyone were to look down from such a lofty height into the sea below they would feel giddy. This is exactly how my soul feels now, as it is raised from the ground by this mighty word of the Lord: 'Blessed are the pure in heart, for they shall see God.'[13]

God offers himself to the vision of those whose hearts have been purified. And yet, as the great John says: 'No one has seen God at any time.'[14] And the sublime mind of Paul confirms this opinion when he says that 'no one has seen or can see God'.[15] God is this slippery, steep crag which yields no footholds for our imagination. Moses too, in his teaching, declares that God is so inaccessible that our mind cannot approach him. He explicitly discourages any attempt to apprehend God, saying: 'No one can see the Lord and live.'[16] To see the Lord is eternal life, and yet these pillars of the faith, John, Paul and Moses, all declare it to be impossible! What vertigo in the soul this causes! Confronted by the abyss of these words I am confounded.

If God is life, then they who do not see God do not see life. On the other hand, the divinely inspired prophets and apostles assert that it is impossible to see God. Is not all human hope thus destroyed? But the Lord supports our faltering hope, just as he grasped Peter when he was in danger of sinking and stood him on the waves as though it were solid ground. If, then, the hand of the Word is extended to us also, supporting those who are at sea in the midst of conflicting speculations, we can be without fear. We are gripped by the guiding hand of the Word who says to us: 'Blessed are the pure in heart, for they shall see God.'

On the Beatitudes, sermon 6.

Blessed are the pure in heart for they shall see God

Those who see God possess in this act of seeing everything that is good: everlasting life, eternal incorruption, unfailing bliss. With these things we shall experience the joy of the eternal kingdom in which happiness is secure; we shall see the true light and hear the delightful voice of the Spirit; we shall exult unceasingly in all that is good in the inaccessible glory of God. This is the magnificent consummation of our hope held out to us by the promise of this Beatitude.

But as I have already suggested, since the seeing is dependent upon our purity of heart, my mind grows dizzy lest it should prove impossible to achieve because what is required of us actually exceeds our capacity . . . What do we gain from knowing that we can see God if at the same time we also know that the mind finds it impossible to do so? It would be just as if someone said that it is blessed to be in heaven because only then can we contemplate what cannot be seen in this life. On the other hand, what if this statement were also pointing out to us the means by which we journey to heaven? Surely it would be valuable for people to know how blessed it is to be there? But then again, as long as the ascent is still declared to be impossible, what is the use of knowing about the bliss of heaven? It only serves to depress those who have learnt about it to realise the things of which they are to be deprived because the ascent is not feasible.

But why should the Lord command something that vastly exceeds our nature and the limits of our power? Surely this is wrong reasoning! God does not instruct those without wings to become birds, nor does he demand those creatures who dwell on the earth to live in the water. The law is adapted to suit the capacities of each in every aspect of life: God never enforces anything contrary to its nature. So we also should realise that nothing is being set forth in this Beatitude that outstrips hope . . .

In trying to penetrate the meaning of the text under consideration, we should note that the Lord does not say that it is blessed to know something about God, but rather to possess God within ourselves: 'Blessed are the pure in heart for they shall see God.' By this I do not think that God presents himself face to face to those who have been purified. Rather I think this marvellous saying teaches us the same thing as the Word expresses in another context: 'The kingdom of God is within you.'[17]

In this saying we learn that if our hearts have been purified of every creature and material sentiment, then we shall see in our own beauty the image of the godhead. In this short sentence the Word, I think, is giving us this advice: there is a desire within you human beings to contemplate the supreme good. When you are told that the majesty of God is exalted far above the heavens, that the divine glory is inexpressible, that its beauty is indescribable, and its nature inaccessible, do not despair at never being able to behold what you desire. It is within your reach; you have in you the ability to see God. For the One who made you also endowed your nature with this marvellous quality. For God imprinted on you the image of his perfection, as the mark of a seal is impressed upon wax. But sin has distorted the imprint of God in you, and this good has become profitless, hidden beneath a covering of filth. You must wash off the dirt that clings to your heart like plaster by a good life, and then the divine beauty will once again shine forth in you.

A similar thing happens with iron. If freed from rust by a whetstone what was one moment black suddenly gleams and glistens in the sunlight. So it is with our inner selves (because this is what our Lord means when he speaks about the 'heart'); once rid of the rustlike dirt that has accumulated by our degenerate behaviour, then we will rediscover our goodness, shining forth in the likeness of our model. For what resembles the Good is in itself good. Hence, when those who are pure of heart look into themselves, they will see the One whom they seek. That is why they are termed blessed, for in gazing at their own translucency they are beholding the model in the image.

Or to give a further analogy: it is just like looking at the sun in a mirror. Even though you do not look directly at the heavens, you do see the sun in the mirror's reflection just as if you were looking directly at it. And so it is with us, says our Lord. Even though we are not strong enough to contemplate the reality of the light, yet if we rediscover the beauty of the image in which we were created at the beginning, then we will find within us what we are seeking.

On the Beatitudes, sermon 6.

Know yourself

Our greatest protection is self-knowledge, and to avoid the delusion that we are seeing ourselves when we are in reality looking at something else. This is what happens to those who do not scrutinize themselves. What they see is strength, beauty, reputation, political power, abundant wealth, pomp, self-importance, bodily stature, a certain grace of form or the like, and they think that this is what they are. Such persons make very poor guardians of themselves: because of their absorption in something else they overlook what is their own and leave it unguarded. How can a person protect what he does not know? The most secure protection for our treasure is to know ourselves: each one must know himself as he is, and distinguish himself from all that he is not, that he may not unconsciously be protecting something else instead of himself.

Commentary on the Song of Songs, sermon 2; ET Musurillo, p.159.

Moses: the servant of the Lord

Many of those who occupy positions of leadership tend to be preoccupied with external appearances. They pay scarce attention to the hidden things of life which are visible only to God. But in the case of Moses this was not so. While he exhorted the Israelites to be of good courage, he cried out to God although outwardly making no sound, as God himself bears witness. The Scriptures teach us, I think, that the voice which is melodious and ascends to God's hearing is not the cry produced by the organs of speech, but the meditation that ascends from a pure conscience . . .

Although Moses was marked out by the various great experiences of his life, he always felt somewhat unfulfilled, restless with desire. He constantly thirsted for that which had already filled him to capacity. He pleaded with God out of a sense of his own inner poverty to give him more, begging God to reveal himself to him not according to his meagre capacity to receive, but as God is in himself. What Moses was experiencing, it seems to me, was a longing which filled his soul for the supreme Good. Hope always draws the soul on from the beauty of that which is seen to that which still lies beyond; and this kindled within Moses a desire to see fully what was now hidden because only partially glimpsed. Thus, the ardent lover of beauty, although constantly the recipient of the visible images, as it were, of what he desires, always longs to be filled with the reality itself. The bold request to climb the mountains of desire is seeking to enjoy the beauty [of God] not in mirrors and reflections, but face to face.

In refusing Moses' request, the voice of God paradoxically grants it, showing in a few words an immeasurable depth of contemplation. The generosity of God granted the fulfilment of Moses' desire, but did not promise that his desire would cease or be fully satisfied. God would not have shown himself to his servant if the sight were such as to bring Moses' desire to behold God to an end. Indeed, the true vision of God consists precisely in this, that a person who looks up to God never ceases to want God. For this reason he says: 'You cannot see my face, for no one can see me and live.'[18] The Scriptures do not mean to suggest by this that the vision of God causes the death of those who enjoy it because how could the face of life ever be the cause of death to those who approach it? On the contrary, God is by nature life-giving. And since God by his very nature transcends all knowledge, it follows that anyone who thinks that God can be understood does not possess life. Such a person has turned away from true Being to an idol of his own creation. True Being is true life, and such Being will always be inaccessible to knowledge . . . God is by his very nature infinite, circumscribed by no boundary.

So what does history have to teach us about this? We are told that 'Moses the servant of the Lord died as the Lord decreed. No one has ever discovered his grave. His eyes were undimmed, and his natural force unimpaired.'[19] From this we learn that when an individual has completed such noble endeavours that person is worthy of a sublime title: 'the servant of the Lord'.[20] Such a title exalts a person far above all others, for in the service of God we become superior to all the world. This for Moses was the culmination of a life of virtue, a culmination wrought through the Word of God . . . What then are we taught through the life of Moses? To have but one purpose in life: to be called 'servants of God' by virtue of the lives we live.

The Life of Moses, 118, 230-235, 314, 317.

The God who makes the darkness his hiding place

Scripture says 'Moses approached the dark cloud where God was.'[21] What does it mean when it says that Moses entered the darkness and then saw God in it? What is now recounted seems somehow to be contradictory to the first theophany,[22] for then the Divine was beheld in light but now is seen in darkness. Let us not think that this is at variance with the sequence of things we have contemplated spiritually. Scripture teaches us by this that religious knowledge comes at first to those who receive it as light. Therefore what is perceived to be contrary to religion is darkness, and the escape from darkness comes about when one participates in light. But as the mind progresses and, through an ever greater and more perfect diligence, comes to apprehend reality, as it approaches more nearly to contemplation, it sees more clearly what of the divine nature is uncontemplated.

For leaving behind everything that is observed, not only what sense comprehends but also what the intelligence thinks it sees, it keeps on penetrating deeper until by the intelligence's yearning for understanding it gains access to the invisible and the incomprehensible, and there it sees God. This is the true knowledge of what is sought; this is the seeing that consists in not seeing, because that which is sought transcends all knowledge, being separated on all sides by incomprehensibility as by a kind of darkness. Wherefore John the sublime, who penetrated into the luminous darkness, says 'No one has ever seen God,'[23] thus asserting that knowledge of the divine essence is unattainable not only by men but also by every intelligent creature.

When, therefore, Moses grew in knowledge, he declared that he had seen God in the darkness, that is, that he had then come to know that what is divine is beyond all knowledge and comprehension, for the text says, 'Moses approached the dark cloud where God was.' What God? The God who [as the Psalmist says] 'made the darkness his hiding place'.[24]

The Life of Moses, 162-164; ET Abraham Malherbe and Everett Ferguson, pp.94-95.

Journey into God

The Lord said to Moses, 'Behold, there is a place with me where you shall stand upon the rock; and while my glory passes by I will put you in a hole in the rock, and I will cover you with my hand until I have passed by; then I will take away my hand, and you shall see my back; but my face shall not be seen.'[25]

What is this place that is said to be with God? What is the meaning of the rock, and what is 'the hole in the rock'? What is the meaning of the 'hand' of the Lord that covers the mouth of the hole of the rock? And what is this 'passing by' of the Lord? And what is the meaning of the 'back' of the Lord, which he promised Moses he would see when Moses had asked to see his face? Each of these details must refer to something of deep importance and worthy of the bounty of the giver. For after all the visions that God's great servant had been given, this promise is believed to be of greater depth and significance. How are we to understand the meaning of this summit to which the text leads us? For it is this which Moses, after so many ascents, longed to reach; and he too helps us to reach it by his guidance who makes 'all things work together for good to those that love God.'[26] 'Behold,' he says, 'there is a place with me.'

I think this idea quite fits all that we have already seen. When God speaks of a place he does not mean a space that can be quantitatively measured – for we cannot measure anything that does not have quantity – but rather by using the analogy of a measurable surface he is guiding the reader to a reality which is infinite and without limit. Here then is something of the meaning of the text as I see it: seeing that you have stretched forth to that which is before you with a great desire, and you never experience complete satisfaction in your progress, nor are you aware of any limit to the good, as your yearning goes out to ever more and more – here is a place with me that is so vast that he who runs in it will never be able to reach the end of his course. And yet, from another point of view, this course has its stability; for God says: 'I will set you on the rock.'

The Life of Moses, 240-244; ET Musurillo, pp.148-149.

On the incarnation

That God should have clothed himself with our nature is a fact that should not seem strange or extravagant to minds that do not form too paltry an idea of reality. Who, looking at the universe, would be so feeble-minded as not to believe that God is all in all; that he clothes himself with the universe, and at the same time contains it and dwells in it? What exists depends on him who exists, and nothing can exist except in the bosom of him who is.

If then all is in him and he is in all, why blush for the faith that teaches us that one day God was born in the human condition, God who still today exists in humanity?

Indeed, if the presence of God in us does not take the same form now as it did then, we can at least agree in recognising that he is in us today no less than he was then. Today, he is involved with us in as much as he maintains creation in existence. Then, he mingled himself with our being to deify it by contact with him, after he had snatched it from death . . . For his resurrection becomes for mortals the promise of their return to immortal life.

Catechetical Orations, 25; ET Olivier Clement, *The Roots of Christian Mysticism*, New City, London, 1993, pp.39-40.

Make me an instrument of peace and reconciliation

'Christ is our peace.'[27] Since Christ is our peace, it is vital that we live up to the name of Christian by allowing Christ to be seen through the way we live, and by allowing his peace to reign in our hearts. As the apostle Paul has said: 'Christ has brought hostility to an end.' So it is incumbent upon us not to allow that hostility to be resuscitated in us in any way at all; we must proclaim its death absolutely. God has destroyed it in a marvellous way for our salvation. Thus it is important that we do not allow ourselves to give way to anger or to nurse grudges because these things will threaten the well-being of our souls. We must not stir to life by our evil actions the very thing that is dead in us.

But because we bear the name of Christ who is peace, we too are called upon to secure the end of all hostility. In this way what we believe with our minds will be professed in our lives. Christ destroyed the dividing wall and brought the two sides together in himself, thus making peace. We too, then, should not only seek to be reconciled with those who attack us externally, we should also be actively seeking to reconcile the warring factions that are fighting within us, so that flesh and spirit are no longer in constant opposition. Then, with our minds stable and our flesh subject to the divine law, we will be refashioned into a unified creature, into men and women of peace. When the two have been made one, we shall experience peace within ourselves. Peace may be defined as a harmony between opposing factions. And so, when the civil war in our nature has been brought to an end and we are at peace with ourselves, then we ourselves will become at peace. Only then can we be true to the name of Christ that we bear.

Treatise on Perfection.

Travelling along the royal highway

The divine law leads us along a royal highway,[28] and the person who has been purified of all desires and passions, will deviate neither to the left nor to the right. And yet how easy it is for a traveller to turn aside from the way. Imagine two precipices forming a high narrow pass; from its centre the person crossing it is in great danger if he veers in either direction because of the chasm on either side that waits to engulf those that stray. In the same way, the divine law requires those who follow its paths not to desert either to left or to right[29] the way which is, as the Lord says, 'narrow and hard'.[30]

This teaching declares that virtue is to be discerned in the mean: evil operates in either a deficiency or in an excess. For example, in the case of courage, cowardice is the product of a lack of virtue, and impetuosity the product of its excess. What is pure and to be identified as virtue is to be discovered in the mean between two contrasting evils. Similarly, other things in life which reach after the good in some strange way follow this middle course between neighbouring evils.

Wisdom clings to the mean between shrewdness and innocence. Neither the wisdom of the serpent nor the innocence of the dove[31] is to be praised if a person opts for one to the neglect of the other. Rather it is the frame of mind that seeks to unite these two attitudes by the mean that constitutes virtue. One person, for example, who lacks moderation becomes self-indulgent; another person whose demands exceed what moderation suggests has his 'conscience seared', as the apostle Paul says.[32] For one has abandoned all restraint in the pursuit of pleasure, and the other ridicules marriage as if it were adultery; whereas the frame of mind formed by the mean of these two attitudes is moderation.

Since, as our Lord says, 'this world is ensnared in wickedness',[33] and everything that is wicked (and therefore opposed to virtue) is alien to those who follow the divine law, it follows that those in this life who pick their way through this world will only reach the destination of their journey in virtue safely if they faithfully keep to the highway which is hardened and smoothed by virtue, and who under no circumstances, will veer aside to explore the byways of evil.

The Life of Moses, 287-290.

NOTES

1   In *The Life of Macrina* Gregory sought to show the way to perfection in a human life, a way which combined culture and holiness, balance and discipline. He also wrote *Dialogue with Macrina on the Soul and the Resurrection* which purports to narrate a conversation he held with his sister on her deathbed. It describes the soul in a process of progressive purification until it attains mystical union with God.

2   Throughout his life Gregory pondered the importance of the monastic life. In spite of being married, he wrote a treatise *On Virginity* in which he developed the idea of interior chastity.

3   Theosebia (or Theosevia) died in about 385, 'a true saint and the true wife of a priest', as a neighbouring bishop said. By this time it was becoming increasingly common for bishops to be celibate.

4   see p.70

5   One of the consequences of Nicene orthodoxy in its reaction to Arianism, was that it drove a theological wedge between God as Creator, and man and the created order. For Origen, the soul's ascent to God had been conceived as a restoration to its original state, a union with its archetype, a movement from darkness and confusion to light and order. For Gregory, there was no natural affinity between the Creator and his creatures; thus the soul's ascent to God is an ascent into the divine darkness.

6   cf. *The Life of Moses*, 273.

7   The three ways were not conceived as successive stages as Origen suggested, but rather as an extended metaphor for understanding the complexity of our spiritual experience.

8   'God made the darkness his hiding place, and his canopy was thick cloud and watery darkness.' Psalm 18: 11; cf. 1 Kings 8: 12.

9   The term was first used in the sixth century by Dionysius in contradistinction to 'cataphatic theology' in which the mind moves progressively towards positive affirmations about the nature of God in relation to creation. Prayer in this tradition is a *via affirmativa*. The theme appeared in Origen and Evagrius, but was not presented as systematically as in Gregory. It is also represented in Western spiritual literature, albeit of a later date, notably *The Cloud of Unknowing* and the works of St John of the Cross.

10   *The Life of Moses*, 165.

11   Romans 11: 33.

12   Psalm 104: 24.

13   Matthew 5: 8.

14   John 1: 18.

15   1 Timothy 6: 16.

16   Exodus 33: 20.

17   Luke 17: 21.

18   Exodus 34: 20.

19   Deuteronomy 34: 5-7.

20   Numbers 12: 7 and Hebrews 3: 15.

21   Exodus 20: 21.

22   Gregory is referring to the appearance at the burning bush.

23   John 1: 18.

24   Psalm 18: 11.

25 Exodus 33: 21-22.
26 Romans 8: 28.
27 Ephesians 2: 14.
28 In company with most of the Fathers, Gregory taught that there is a *via regia*, a
    'royal highway' to be travelled in life. This language first appeared with the
    Jewish writer Philo (c.20BC to c.AD50). In Christian contexts the language
    resonated with the earliest metaphor for Christian discipleship. According to
    Luke (Acts 11: 26), it was at Antioch that the name 'Christian' was first used of
    the disciples of Jesus of Nazareth; previously, they had been known merely as
    followers of 'the Way'. Gradually, this dynamic language evolved into an image
    of the continuity of the Christian tradition: it signalled a living wisdom about
    how to live out the demands of the Gospel in the complexity of daily life.
    In this passage Gregory (following Clement of Alexandria) identified the 'royal
    highway' of the virtues as the 'narrow gate' of the Gospels which passes
    between extremes. For Gregory, there was no set formula for being a Christian
    in the world, only a way of travelling through life with integrity and discernment.
29 Deuteronomy 28: 14; Isaiah 30: 21.
30 Matthew 7: 14.
31 Matthew 10: 16.
32 1 Timothy 4: 2.
33 1 John 5: 19.

SELECT BIBLIOGRAPHY

TEXTS and TRANSLATIONS
PG 44-46.
Gregorii Nysseni opera, critical edition W. Jaeger and H. Langerbeck, Leiden, 1964.
The Life of Moses, ET with notes Abraham Malherbe and Everett Ferguson, Paulist
    Press, New York, 1978.
From Glory to Glory: Texts from Gregory of Nyssa, selected and introduced Jean
    Danielou, ET and edited Herbert Musurillo, John Murray, London, 1962.
Sermons on the Lord's Prayer and the Beatitudes, edited and ET H. Graef, ACW 18.

STUDIES
Lossky, V., (ET) *The Mystical Theology of the Eastern Church*, James Clarke,
    Cambridge, 1957/1973.
Louth, A., *The Origins of the Christian Mystical Tradition*, Clarendon Press, Oxford,
    1981.

5

John Chrysostom
SOCIAL JUSTICE AND THE PRAYER OF PROTEST

*'Nothing is colder than a Christian who does not
care for the salvation of others.'*

HOMILY 20 ON THE ACTS OF THE APOSTLES

John Chrysostom was born in Antioch, the third city of the Roman
empire, in about 347. He was born into a wealthy family and he carried
the self-assurance of his background and status throughout his life. His
father, a military commander, died when John was still a child, and as a
result he was brought up almost entirely by his mother, a devout Christian.
John was educated for the law under the great pagan orator Libanius, but in
368 he received baptism, renounced his career as an advocate, and devoted
himself single-mindedly to Biblical study and the ascetic life. At some point,
desirous of a more perfect life, he left home and lived as a hermit in a cave;
but after two years returned to the city, exhausted. In 381 he was made
deacon and served at Antioch under Bishop Flavian. Five years later he was
ordained priest, in preparation for which he wrote his treatise *On the
Priesthood*, in which he brings out the sacrificial meaning of that service. It
was Bishop Flavian who gave John responsibility for preaching. We need
to remember that in the early centuries the ministry of preaching was almost
invariably reserved to the bishop; so this was an exceptional mark of
recognition. Indeed, John's oratorical brilliance earned him in the sixth
century the surname 'Chrysostom' which literally means 'golden-mouthed'.

During the years 386-398 when his powers of oratory were at their
highest – sometimes he preached for two hours at a time – John delivered

103

numerous homilies on Genesis, Matthew, John, and the Pauline Epistles. Paul was his favourite author whom he read and re-read. His output was prodigious: over seven hundred homilies have survived. In common with the theological tradition of biblical scholarship at Antioch, he disliked the allegorical interpretation of Scripture, always insisting that the Bible be interpreted literally. This radical attention to the text was matched by an equally radical application of the Word to society.

In the decades that followed the persecutions, the nominally Christian populace that now thronged the doors of the Church was creating a sense of mounting frustration within the Church. It was this climate of discontent and ferment that formed the backcloth for much of John's preaching. For example, he was particularly disgusted at the indifference of the rich and powerful to the plight of the urban and rural poor. His sermons were often angry, laced with calls for social justice, with demands for the liberation of slaves, for an end to the exploitation of peasants and the appropriation of their land. He praised a communion of goods, issuing a summons to individual and collective sharing. His exegesis of St Matthew chapter 25 led him to a sacramental view of all life: the poor man like the priest is 'another Christ'; the 'sacrament of the altar' must be carried out 'into the street' by the 'sacrament of the brother'. Few pastors have discerned more clearly than John that the eucharistic fellowship in which poor, wealthy, slave and citizen alike participate, requires expression not simply in charity, but in social justice. Although John stopped short of articulating a coherent Christian political theory, he was not afraid to goad his hearers' consciences. His critique of society, his stinging rebukes of hypocrisy, and his repeated call for integrity in discipleship, are as challenging to his readers today as they must have been to his contemporaries.

Chrysostom's fame as a preacher spread, and against his wish in 398 he was made Patriarch of Constantinople, the new imperial city. In the capital he won his people's hearts, he increased the number of hospitals, and evangelised the surrounding countryside. He set about the task of reforming the higher clergy, exposing corruption, and challenging complacency both in the Church and at court. He denounced luxury and the insatiable appetite for power as an insult to the poverty and powerlessness of ordinary people. 'Mules bear fortunes and Christ dies of hunger at your gate,' he is alleged to have cried out. But the vehemence of his language, his rigid asceticism, his political naivety and often sheer tactlessness (unlike Ambrose in Milan, John Chrysostom was no diplomat!) soon brought him into conflict with a large section of the clergy, with a powerful section at court, and above all with the Empress Eudoxia. Not without reason, she took Chrysostom's invective as a personal assault upon herself.

With the help of Theophilus, the disgruntled and jealous Patriarch of Alexandria who despised Chrysostom and consistently tried to undermine him, the Empress contrived to have a special Synod convened at which various spurious charges were brought against Chrysostom. He was condemned and deposed from his see and threatened with exile. The people of Constantinople, however, were so outraged at this decision that the authorities bowed to popular pressure and had him recalled. Sadly (but also predictably), the truce was short-lived. Within two months, Chrysostom's plain speaking had precipitated a further confrontation with the Empress which this time proved definitive. In 404 he was abducted in the middle of celebrating Easter. In spite of the support of the populace and the intervention of Pope Innocent I of Rome, Chrysostom was banished. The last extract in this selection is part of the homily he preached to the people before he left the city. It stands as one of the most moving pieces of oratory in the history of Christian preaching, and is testimony to the stature and personal integrity of this tragic man.

Initially, he was exiled to Cucusa in Lower Armenia, but when after three years it became clear that, in spite of his broken health, he would not die there soon enough, he was made to travel on foot in unsuitable weather conditions to the fortress of Arabissos at the eastern end of the Black Sea. He never arrived. The combination of exposure, near starvation, accumulated strain and physical exhaustion killed him. He died in September 407, saying: 'Glory be to God for everything.' He was sixty years old.

Consider your call

The cross brought conviction to the world and drew the whole world to itself through the work of uneducated people. They succeeded not by preaching trivia, but by speaking of God, of true religion, of a way of living the Gospel, and of the coming judgement. It turned peasants and illiterate folk alike into philosophers. See how the foolishness of God is wiser than human wisdom, and his weakness stronger! In what way was it stronger? It was stronger because it turned the world upside down; it gripped people, and although countless individuals were busy trying to suppress the name of the Crucified, they only succeeded in promoting its cause. It flourished and grew; by contrast, they perished and withered away. The living who were fighting him who had died proved powerless. And so, when the Greek tells me that I am a fool, all that he is doing is revealing his own foolishness. He thinks me a fool, but in reality I am wiser than the wise. When he ridicules me as being weak, he only demonstrates his own greater weakness. For by the grace of God, tax collectors and fishermen had the strength to achieve noble things, such things as neither monarchs nor orators nor philosophers, in a word, not the entire world searching in every direction, could even imagine . . .

Reflecting on this, Paul said: 'The weakness of God is stronger than human strength.'[1] It is clear from this as well that the Gospel is divine. For how else could twelve illiterate men have been inspired to attempt such enormous feats, men who lived on the banks of lakes or rivers, or in deserts? How else could it have occurred to these men, men who had scarcely ventured into a city or the forum, to take on the entire world? It is apparent from the Gospel narratives that they were cowardly and timid. The Scriptures never attempt to make excuses for them or to cover up their failings. In itself this is compelling evidence of the truth. What then does the Gospel say about them? That after the innumerable miracles they had seen Christ perform, when he was arrested, some of them fled, and the one disciple who stayed behind denied him, and he was chief among them!

So then, here we have people who failed to stand up to the Jews when Christ was alive; and yet no sooner was Christ dead and buried, than they take on the whole world. How can this be unless Christ rose from the dead, talked with them and put fresh heart into them? If it were not so, would they have not have said to themselves: What is all this? If Christ did not have the strength to save himself, how can he protect us? He did not defend himself when he was alive, so will he reach out his hand to defend us now that he is dead? When he was alive he did not conquer a single nation, so how shall we convince the entire world by speaking his name?

Would it not have been foolish to conceive of such an enterprise, let alone actually to do it? Surely it is obvious that if the disciples had not seen Jesus risen from the dead and received clear evidence of his power, they would never have risked such a gamble.

Homily 4 on the first Epistle to the Corinthians, 3, 4.

Let your light so shine

In my view there is nothing so cold as a Christian who does not care about the salvation of other people. It is useless to plead poverty in this respect for the poor widow who put two copper coins [in the treasury] will be your accuser.[2] And remember, Peter said, 'Silver and gold have I none,'[3] and Paul was so poor that he often went hungry and without the basic necessities of life. Nor can you plead humble birth because the apostles were of humble origin and from obscure families. You cannot claim lack of education because they too were illiterate ... You cannot plead sickness either because Timothy suffered poor health and was often ill.[4] ... Everyone can be of service to their neighbour if only we exercise our responsibilities.

Look at the trees of the forest. See how sturdy they are, how beautiful, how tall, and how smooth their bark; but they do not bear fruit. If we had a garden we would prefer to plant pomegranates or olive trees. The other trees may be delightful to look at but they are not grown for profit, or if they are, it is very small. People who are concerned only for themselves are like those trees of the forest – no, they are not even as worthwhile. At least forest timber can be used for building houses and fortifications, whereas they are good only for the bonfire. They are like the foolish virgins [in the parable]: chaste certainly, discreet and modest too, but of service to no one.[5] That is why they were cast out. Such is the fate of those who do not nourish Christ.

You should reflect on the fact that none is charged with specific sins such as fornication or perjury; they are charged simply with being of no service to their fellow men and women. Take the example of the man who went and buried his talent.[6] He led a blameless life but a life that was not of service to others. How can such a person be called a Christian? If yeast when it is mixed with the flour fails to leaven the dough, how can it be called yeast? Or again, if a perfume cannot be sensed by those present, how can it be called perfume in any meaningful sense? So do not say, 'I cannot encourage others to become Christians; it is impossible;' because if you were really a Christian, it would be impossible for you not to do so.

In the natural world, the way things behave is an expression of their properties. It is the same situation here: what I am describing belongs to the very nature of being a Christian. So do not insult God. To claim that the sun cannot shine or that a Christian cannot do good is equally insulting, and to call God a liar ... Once we get our lives ordered, however, then the rest will follow as a natural consequence. It is impossible for the light of a Christian to be hidden; it is impossible for so resplendent a lamp to be concealed.

Homily 20 on the Acts of the Apostles, 4.

Social justice

God delivered up his Son; so why is it, my friends, that you refuse to give even a morsel of bread to Christ who was delivered up for you and killed for you? For your sake the Father did not spare him although he was his only Son. You, however, despise Christ when he is pining with starvation although the cost to you is not only met out of an account that has been put into credit by Christ, but your action would also gain you further interest. He was delivered up for you and killed for you. He wandered around hungry for you. You have only to give away something of his in order to receive the benefit yourself; and yet even this you refuse to do.

How senseless, harder than flint, are such people who, in spite of so much encouragement, are locked into a pattern of brutal cruelty! Christ did not think it sufficient to undergo the cross and death. He willed to become the pauper in our midst, a stranger, a beggar, a tramp, a prisoner and a sick man, so that at least by this means he might draw you to himself. 'If you do not pay me back,' he says, 'as the one who suffered for you, then at least take pity on me in my poverty. If you do not pity me in my poverty, then have compassion on me in my sickness and be gentle on account of my imprisonment. If even these things cannot stir you to charity, then reflect what a small thing it is that I am asking of you. I am not asking for anything expensive, only for something to eat, for shelter and for a few words of comfort. If you are still hard-hearted, then I beg you to change for the sake of the kingdom of heaven and for the rewards that I have promised you; or does all this mean nothing to you?'

'At any rate be moved by a natural compassion when you see me with hardly a rag to cover my body; remember how I was naked on the cross for you. If the nakedness of the poor leaves you untouched, then remember mine. Now, as then, I am in bonds for you. Show me some mercy when you reflect upon either my current sufferings or my former sufferings. Once I fasted for you; and now, once again, I am hungry for your sake. When I hung upon the cross I suffered thirst; now I suffer thirst again in my poor. All that I have done, all that I am continuing to do, is meant to draw you to myself, to make you charitable, and to secure your own salvation.'

'I am asking you to repay me for the countless benefits I have bestowed on you. I am not demanding it as if you were in debt to me: I want to crown your generosity and give you a kingdom in exchange for mere trifles. I am not asking you to abolish my poverty or to give me wealth, even though I became poor for you. I am only asking for a crust of bread, for some clothes, and some relief in my hunger. If I am thrown into prison, I am not insisting that you secure my release; I am only asking that you come and visit me as one who was bound for you. This will be sufficient for me, and in return I will give you heaven. Although I have released you from the worst possible prison, it will be sufficient for me if you come and visit me in prison.'

'I could crown you without all this; but you see, I wish to be in your debt, so that the crown gives you some sense of affirmation. I come among you begging; I stand at your door and stretch out my hand to you; for though in truth I am able to support myself, I wish to be supported by you. For I love you above all else, and I long to eat at your table, for that is the mark of those who love.'

Homily 15 on the Epistle to the Romans, 6.

Be discerning Christians

Do you want to honour the body of Christ? Then do not despise his nakedness. Do not honour him here [in church] clothed in silk vestments and then ignore him, naked and frozen in the street. Always remember that he who said, 'This is my body', and gave effect to his word, also said, 'I was hungry and you gave me no food', and 'inasmuch as you did not do it to one of these, you did not do it to me'.[7] The body of Christ needs no clothing in the first sense but only [the worship of] a pure heart. But in the second case it needs clothing and all the care we can lavish upon it.

It is vital, therefore, that we become discerning Christians and learn to honour Christ appropriately in ways of which he approves. When someone is honoured the form of honour bestowed is appropriate to the person receiving it, not the donor. Peter thought he was honouring the Lord when he tried to prevent him from washing his feet, but in reality this was far from the case. In the same way give God the honour he seeks and give your money generously to the poor. God does not need golden cups but he does need golden hearts.

I am not saying that you should not donate golden chalices, but I am insisting that there is no substitute for almsgiving. The Lord will not refuse your gift but he prefers almsgiving; and inevitably so, because in the former case only you, the donor benefits, whereas in the latter case the poor benefit. The gift of a chalice may be extravagant; the giving of alms is sincere kindness which shows love for our fellow men and women.

What is the point of weighing down Christ's table with golden chalices while he himself is starving? Feed the hungry and then, if you have any money left over, lavish his table. Will you fashion a cup of gold and withhold a cup of water? What use is it to adorn his table with hangings of cloth of gold but refuse Christ a coat for his back? What gain is to be had from such behaviour? Answer me this question: if you saw someone starving and refused to give them any food but instead spent your money on covering Christ's table with gold, would Christ thank you for it? Would he not rather be furious with you? Or again, if you saw someone in rags and frozen stiff, and then instead of giving them clothing you went and erected golden columns in Christ's honour, would not Christ say that you were mocking and ridiculing him? Imagine that Christ is that tramp, that stranger who comes in need of a bed for the night. You turn him away and then start laying carpets on the floor, draping the walls, hanging lamps on silver chains from the capitals of the columns. Meanwhile the tramp is arrested and put in prison, but you never give him a second thought.

Let me repeat, I am not condemning generosity; but I am urging you to care for the poor; indeed, to give the poor priority. No one was ever condemned for not beautifying Christ's house, but those who neglect their neighbour were threatened with hell fire and eternal punishment with devils. Beautify this house if that is what you want to do, but never neglect your brother or sister in need. They are temples of infinitely greater value.

Homily 50 on the Gospel according to Matthew, 4.

Be wise as serpents but innocent as doves

If we always behave as sheep, we will be victorious. Even if ten thousand wolves prowl around us, we will overcome and be victorious. But the moment we become wolves, we ourselves will be conquered because we will forfeit the help of our shepherd. For he is the shepherd of sheep, not of wolves. If he abandons you and goes away it is because you refuse to allow him to display his power . . .

Listen to his words: 'Be not dismayed that I send you out among wolves and bid you be like sheep and like doves. I could have done the opposite, and not allowed you to suffer any hurt. I could have prevented you from being the victims of wolves and made you fiercer than lions; but I have chosen a better way. The way that I have chosen gives you glory and proclaims my power.' Listen to these words addressed to Paul: 'My grace is sufficient for you, for my power is made perfect in weakness.'[8] That is the way I made you.

So when [Christ] says: 'I am sending you out like sheep,' he is in effect saying: 'Do not despair, for I know that in this way, more than any other, you will in fact be invincible against all your enemies.' He is wanting us to make some effort of our own so that everything will not seem to come from grace.[9] He does not want it to appear as if our crown was not earned, and so he says: 'Be wise as serpents and innocent as doves.' What power, he asks, does wisdom have in such circumstances? How can we exercise wisdom at all when we are engulfed by such tempests? However wise the sheep may be, when they are surrounded by wolves, and the wolves are as numerous as the sheep, what can wisdom achieve? However innocent the dove may be, what advantage is its innocence when it is harried by so many hawks? Of course, in the case of irrational animals, the answer is none at all; but in the case of human beings, then the answer is quite a lot!

But first, let us think about the kind of wisdom that is being demanded of us. Christ calls it the wisdom 'of a serpent'. The serpent abandons everything – even if its body is severed, it does not resist much, provided it can save its head. In the same way, Jesus is saying abandon everything except your faith, even if it means giving up your wealth, your body, life itself. Your faith is your head and your roots. If you preserve that, though you lose all else in life, you will receive everything back again with even greater glory. That is why our Lord commanded that we should be not merely simple and honest, nor merely wise; but he forged the two qualities into virtue. A person should have the wisdom of the serpent so as not to receive mortal wounds. But a person should also display the innocence of a dove so as not to retaliate against those who wrong us or take our revenge on those who try to undermine us. By itself wisdom is useless unless it is accompanied by innocence. What is more demanding than such commandments? After all, is it not enough to have to suffer wrong? No, says Christ, it is not enough. I do not even permit you to bear a grudge ... Nobody should think that these commandments are impossible to fulfil. More than anyone else, Christ understands human nature. Violence, he knows, is not overcome by violence, but by gentleness.

Homily 33 on the Gospel according to Matthew, 1, 2.

God explores the secret intentions of the heart

Let each of us, with an informed conscience, enter into a review of our actions, and bring our whole life before our minds for assessment and try to discern whether we are deserving of correction or punishment. When we are indignant that somebody whom we reckon guilty of various crimes escapes with impunity, let us first reflect upon our own faults, and perhaps our indignation will cease. Crimes appear great because they usually involve great or notorious matters; but once we inquire into our own actions, we will perhaps find numerous other matters for concern.

For example, to steal or to defraud a person is the same thing: the gravity of the offence is not lessened by whether it is gold or silver that is at stake. In either case it is the attitude of mind that is the root cause. A person who steals a small object will not baulk at the chance of stealing something bigger. If he does not steal, it is probably because he lacks the opportunity. A poor man who robs a poorer person would not hesitate to rob the rich given half the chance. His forebearance issues simply from weakness, not from choice. You say to me: 'That ruler is robbing his subjects.' But tell me now, do you not steal from others yourselves? It is no use you objecting that he is stealing vast sums of money whereas you are taking only a little. [Reflect upon the incident in the Gospel where] the widow gave two copper coins to charity and in so doing acquired as much merit as rich people who offered gold. Why was that? It was because God sees the intentions of the heart and is not interested in quantity. If that applies to almsgiving . . . why should not the same criteria apply to wrongful dealings? Just as the widow who offered two coppers was considered equal to the greatest benefactor, thanks to her good intention, so you who steal even two coppers are as guilty as thieves who rob on a bigger scale.

Homily 3 on the second Epistle to Timothy, 3.

The battlefield of the heart

Christ has showed you the true light. If you shun it and retreat again into the darkness, what will be your excuse? What sort of allowance can be made for you? . . . 'I am the victim of the violence that lurks within my nature,' you say. 'I love Christ, but my nature compels me to sin.' If you are under some sort of compulsion to sin, if you are the victim of inner violence, then allowance will indeed be made. On the other hand, if you are sinning through indolence, then expect no leniency. So let us explore this issue to see if we commit sins by compulsion, under pressure of violence, rather than through indolence or negligence.

The Law states: 'You shall not kill.' Who compels you to kill? Who forces you to do it? Is it not rather the case that you have to do violence to yourself in order to kill someone? Which of us here would casually cut our neighbour's throat? Who would willingly stain their hands with blood? No one. So the reality is the exact opposite of what you claim: to sin, you have to force yourself.

God has bestowed upon human nature the gift of mutual love as a result of which 'every living creature is capable of loving its own kind, and every human being is capable of loving their neighbour.'[10] Do you understand? Our nature predisposes us to virtue. It is the vices that are contrary to our nature. If they are victorious it will be the result of our own negligence. Take another example: adultery; what shall we say about that? What sort of compulsion drives you to that? You answer: 'The tyranny of lust.' But why? I ask. Why cannot you have sexual intercourse with your spouse and defeat this tyranny? But you reply 'But I am consumed with passion for someone else's spouse.' In that case there is no compulsion. Love cannot be compelled. You do not love because you have been forced to love someone: you love out of deliberate free choice, of your own free will. Sexual intercourse may be a very powerful craving, but to love someone else's partner is a matter of free choice.

Homily 2 on the Epistle to the Ephesians, 3.

Learn how to give

It is not enough to give [to the poor]: we must give to them with generosity and without grumbling. It is not even enough to give without grumbling: we must give gladly and willingly . . . [When the poor are helped] two conditions ought always to be evident: generosity and joy.

Why do you moan about having to give something [to charity]? Why do you display such resentment in giving alms? If you resent almsgiving, you are showing no mercy; you expose merely your callousness and lack of humanity. If you are full of resentment, how exactly are you going to help someone who is in the pit of depression? Afterwards you will be happy when you see that they are neither demeaned nor humiliated because you have helped them joyfully. Nothing causes embarrassment so much as having to be beholden to others. But by showing joy when you give you will enable your brother or sister to overcome their suspicion. They will realise that in your own estimation, you are receiving yourself in the process of giving. On the other hand, if you show resentment, far from raising their spirits, you will succeed only in depressing them still further. That is why Paul says: 'Let he who gives, do so cheerfully.'[11]

If you give gladly, even if it be only a small thing, it can be munificent. If you give unwillingly, even if you give substantially, it will turn into a pittance. It is the attitude of the giver that determines the assessment of our deeds.

Homily 21 on the Epistle to the Romans, 1.

Christian marriage

Marriage is a mystery and a sign of an important truth. 'It is a mystery,' says Paul, 'and I understand it in relation to Christ and his Church.'[12] ... It is a mystery, and the mystery consists in this: the two spouses are united and the two become one. [As at the Incarnation] at the entrance of the Word [into the created order] there was no ceremony or noise, but a great silence, a quiet tranquillity;[13] in the same way, two people come together and are united not in a lifeless image, not even in an image drawn from this world, but in the image of God himself . . . They form one body. What a mystery of love! . . .

There is no human relationship so intimate as that between husband and wife, if they are united as they should be . . . It is why Paul spent so much effort in speaking of this subject and why he says: 'Wives, be subject to your husbands as you are to the Lord.'[14] From these words of Paul you sense how absolute should be a wife's subjection to her husband . . . But now listen to what Paul also requires of husbands, for he employs an identical argument: 'Husbands, love your wives as Christ loved the Church.'[15] You see the measure of obedience that is asked; hear also how much love is required. You husbands want your wives to obey you as the Church obeys Christ? Then you must care for them as much as Christ cares for the Church. Should it be necessary for you to die for your wife, to be cut into ten thousand pieces, to endure and undergo any suffering whatever, you should never refuse. And even if you were to suffer, you would still have done nothing when compared with what Christ has done for you. Indeed, you would be doing things for someone to whom you are already united, whereas Christ did them for us in the face of our opposition and hatred of him; we abused him, we spat at him, and finally rejected him. He used no threats or violence; he never resorted to humiliation or fear; but with unwearying tenderness, Christ wooed his Church in love.[16] You too, must behave towards your wives in the same way. Even if you perceive that she despises you, even if she rejects and humiliates you, you can bring her back to you if you cherish her, if you care for her, if you are tender to her, if you love her.

Nothing is stronger than bonds of love, particularly between husband and wife. By resorting to intimidation you might succeed in keeping a domestic servant attached to you; but in all probability the servant will leave you and run away. But the companion of your life, the mother of your children, the ground of your joy, ought she be tied to you by threats and fear? Surely, by love and cherishing? What sort of union would it be where the wife was petrified of her husband? And what pleasure could her husband find in tyrannising her as if she were a slave instead of respecting her as a free woman? . . .

Two souls united in love should have nothing to fear either in the present or the future. For when there is harmony, peace and a mutuality of love, then husband and wife already possess everything that is good. No preoccupation should vex them and they should be able to live with integrity behind the impregnable fortress that protects them which is nothing less than a harmony in conformity with God. Their marriage will be harder than diamonds and tougher than iron. They are walking with a firm step on the road that leads to eternal life, and in so doing, they will enjoy a continual increase in divine grace.

Homily 12 on the Epistle to the Colossians, 5.
Homily 20 on the Epistle to the Ephesians, 1.
Homily 38 on Genesis, 7.

Celebrating creation

God has made this world beautiful, glorious, varied, and rich. He has made it capable of meeting your every need, to nourish your body and to develop the life of your soul by leading it towards the knowledge of himself – and all this, for your sake. For you he has made the sky radiant with stars. He has embellished it with sun and moon so that you can rejoice in it and profit by it . . .

In every corner of the earth there are trees growing. It is impossible to study all their species: their fruit, their use, their fragrance, their appearance, their character, their leaves, their colour, their shape, their height or smallness, the way to find them, to preserve them or to cultivate them, the variety of bark, their girth and branches, the healing properties that many of them possess; but all exist for you.

In the same way the arts are for you; cities, countryside, sleep is for you; death is for you and life is for you. This magnificent world exists for you. And it will also exist for you tomorrow when it becomes better. For without doubt it will become better, and it will become specially so for you. Listen to what Paul says: 'The creation itself will be set free from its bondage to decay', that is from its corruptibility. And it will obtain this privilege, this honour because of you. That is why Paul goes on to say: 'the glorious liberty of the children of God.'

The providence of God shines with greater strength than the light of this world. So do not examine events that are above you or scrutinise God's motives which you cannot fathom. For your very existence has been given you out of pure generosity. God has no need of our help. Let us rather marvel and give God the glory.

On Providence, 7, 2; 31.

For me, life is Christ and death is gain

The waves have risen and the surging sea is dangerous, but we do not fear drowning for we stand upon the rock. Let the sea surge! It cannot destroy the rock. Let the waves rise! They cannot sink the boat of Jesus. Tell me, what are we to fear? Is it death? But 'for me life is Christ, and death is gain.'[17] So tell me, is it exile? 'The earth is the Lord's and all that it contains.'[18] Is it the confiscation of property? 'We brought nothing into the world and it is certain we can take nothing out of it.'[19] I have nothing but contempt for the threats of this world; its treasures I ridicule. I am not afraid of poverty, I do not crave after wealth, I am not afraid of death, and I do not seek to live except it be of help to you. So I simply mention my present circumstances and call on you, my dear people, to remain steadfast in your love.

Do you not hear the Lord saying: 'Where two or three are gathered together in my name, there I am among them'?[20] Where will he be absent, for where will there not be two or three bound together by love? I have his pledge, so I do not have to rely on my own strength. I cling to his promise: it is my staff, my security, it is my peaceful harbour. Even though the entire world be in turmoil, I cling to his promise and read it. It is my rampart and my shield. What promise is this? 'I am with you always, even to the end of time.'[21]

Christ is with me, whom shall I fear? Let the waves rise up against me, the seas, the wrath of rulers: these things to me are mere cobwebs. And if you, my dear people, had not held me back I would have left this very day. I always say, 'Lord, your will be done'; not what this person or that person wishes, but as you wish. This is my fortress, this is my immovable rock, this is my firm staff. If God wishes this to be, then so be it. If he wishes me to be here, I thank him. Wherever he wants me to be, I thank him. Wherever I am, there are you also; where you are, there am I too; we are one body. And the body cannot be separated from its head, nor the head from the rest of the body. We may be separated by space, but we are united by love. Not even death can sever us. For even if my body dies, my soul will live on, and my soul will remember you, my people.

You are my fellow-citizens, my fathers, my brothers, my children, my limbs, my body, my light, and yes, dearer to me than light. For what can the rays of the sun give me when compared with the gift of your love? Its rays are useful to me in this present life, but your love is weaving for me a crown for the life that is to come.

Before his exile, 1-3.

NOTES

1   1 Corinthians 1: 25.
2   Luke 21: 4.
3   Acts 3: 6.
4   1 Timothy 5: 23.
5   Matthew 25: 1-13.
6   Matthew 25: 24.
7   Matthew 25: 45.
8   2 Corinthians 12: 9.
9   John Chrysostom in company with other Greek theologians, did not have as low an opinion of human nature and its potential for good, as became prevalent in the West. His writing stands in sharp contrast to that of Augustine who taught that humanity is unable even to will what is good without the grace of God. The Greek Fathers taught a doctine of *synergia*, of 'joint energies', of God and humanity working in co-operation. It was a theology which tried to respect human dignity without detracting from the sovereignty of grace.
10   Ecclesiasticus 8: 15.
11   Romans 12: 8.
12   Ephesians 5: 32.
13   Chrysostom's language here is drawing upon Scripture: 'When all things were lying in tranquillity and silence, and night had run half of her swift course, from the royal throne, leapt down your mighty Word.' (Wisdom 18:14,15) This text was interpreted by the Fathers as expressive of the incarnation and from an early date it appears in liturgical contexts; indeed, the text is still used as a Christmas antiphon. Here Chrysostom is saying that the union between husband and wife is of the highest order: it is a reflection of the grace and stability of the Word made flesh.
14   Ephesians 5: 22.
15   Ephesians 5: 25.
16   literally 'brought her to lie at his feet.'
17   Philippians 1: 21.
18   Psalm 24: 1.
19   1 Timothy 6: 7.
20   Matthew 18: 20.
21   Matthew 28: 20.

SELECT BIBLIOGRAPHY

TEXTS and TRANSLATIONS
PG 47, 48, 49, 51, 53, 54, 56, 58, 60-3.
Critical ed. and introduction to specific works (together with French translation) SC, 13, 28, 50, 79, 117, 125, 138, 188, 272, 277, 300.
No complete ET of Chrysostom's works exists, but the principal works are available in a rather dated translation in NPNF 9-14.

STUDIES
Attwater, D., *St John Chrysostom*, Collins, London, 1960.
Baur, C. *John Chrysostom and his Time*, 2 vols. Newman Press, Westminster MD, 1959-60.
Spidlik, T., (ET) *The Spirituality of the Christian East: A Systematic Handbook*, Cistercian Studies, Kalamazoo, Michigan, 1985.

6

Augustine
DRAWN BY LOVE

'My weight is my love: wherever I go, it is love that draws me.'
CONFESSIONS

ugustine is rightly acclaimed one of the greatest minds that have
ever lived, and his formative influence upon the development of
Western thought is difficult to overestimate. He was born in 354 in
Thagaste in Numidia (what is now Algeria), the son of a pagan father,
Patrick, and a devout Christian mother, Monica. By temperament, he was
passionate and sensual. As a young man he rejected the Christianity of his
mother in favour of Manicheism,[1] one of the great universalist religions of
his day with an appeal not dissimilar to that of contemporary 'New Age'
philosophies. But after nine years he became disillusioned and abandoned
it: it failed to deal adequately with the problem of evil or give Augustine the
intellectual satisfaction which he craved.

His career as an orator and rhetorician led him from Carthage to Rome,
and from there to Milan where the Imperial Court at that time resided. It was
in Milan that Augustine heard Ambrose preach, and as a result, began to
explore the Christian Scriptures afresh. Hitherto, their crude Latin
translations which compared so unfavourably with the classical elegance of,
for example, Cicero, had led him to discount their worth. Augustine's
knowledge of Greek was at best modest. In his *Confessions* we learn how
sitting in the garden of his villa one day, depressed and dejected, Augustine
heard the laughter of children with their hypnotic chant: '*tolle, lege*' – 'take
it up and read!' – and how in these words he discerned the divine invitation
to study the Scriptures. It proved to be the germination point of a
distinctively biblical spirituality.

123

Augustine was baptised by Ambrose at the Easter Vigil on 23 April 387. It is this event that forms the climax of the *Confessions*. Two extracts from the work are included in this anthology. It is a sort of spiritual autobiography in which Augustine recounts his searching for truth, his anguish, and the various steps that led to his conversion. He describes how he came to the realisation that the spiritual life is a grace with which a person must co-operate, not a prize to be captured or a trophy to be won. The book was highly influential, but also somewhat scandalous – at least to Augustine's fellow North African Christians whose piety and sense of moral rectitude were well known. In it Augustine informs his readers that he had had a common law wife and had had a child by her. But it would be wrong to sensationalise this aspect of Augustine's life: the *Confessions* are more than an acknowledgement of past error or moral impotence. They are a declaration of faith in Christ as the Word and Wisdom of God, the goal of the human search for truth. Above all, they are a confession of praise. The spirituality of Augustine displays this recurrent three-fold theme: penitence, faith, and praise.

Augustine returned to North Africa in 388. In the course of the journey his mother died. It was a devastating blow. Augustine had been very close to his mother; indeed, Monica had been as instrumental in her son's conversion as Ambrose. In 396 Augustine became bishop of Hippo, a big, commercial port and the second diocese in Africa after Carthage. Sadly, the city was in turmoil because of the Donatist schism.[2] There were two Christian communities with rival bishops and churches, and violence had erupted. This was the background to Augustine's tireless plea for unity and peace in the Church of God. But the controversy which called forth his greatest intellectual energies was Pelagianism.

Pelagius was a British monk living in Rome who preached vigorously against what he perceived as moral laxity and decadence in the society around him. In his preaching, however, it would seem that he tended to overstate the human capacity for change and renewal – invariably at the expense of divine grace – and conversely (and ironically), to underestimate the corporate dimension of sin and its corrosive effect on society. It would appear that he was naively optimistic about what was possible for an individual to achieve. In response Augustine criticised Pelagius's analysis of the human predicament as simplistic. Not surprisingly, his own life-experience had led him to a more pessimistic and (many would claim) realistic view of humanity's potential for change.[3] For Augustine, repentance marked the triumph of grace in a person's life. It was Augustine's view that humankind is not as free as it thinks: wills are flawed, paralysed, and need to be set free by God's grace. This emphasis on the sovereignty of grace runs like a silver thread throughout Augustine's writings.

Augustine's literary works comprise around one hundred titles. In addition to the *Confessions*, his treatises *On the Trinity* and *The City of God* are his two most important works. Excerpts from both are included here. In the former, Augustine discovered in human psychology (in the inter-play of memory, understanding and will) and in the nature of love itself analogies with which to understand the mystery of the Holy Trinity. 'If I knew myself,' argued Augustine, 'I would know God' (*noverim me, noverim te*). The search for God and self is created in the image of God and is therefore receptive to God (*copax Dei*). It was his belief that our desire for God invigorates and expands our capacity to welcome and receive God into our lives until, by grace, we come to share in the intimacy of love which is the life of the blessed Trinity.

In *The City of God*, written against a background of fear and confusion following the sack of Rome by Alaric the Goth in 410, Augustine took up the challenge of the pagans who claimed that this tragedy was a direct consequence of the people abandoning their ancient gods (who alone were deemed capable of defending the empire) in favour of Christianity. The accusation was both insidious and subtle, not least because some Christians had constructed an apology for their faith on the premise that the future of the empire would be secure as long as it remained Christian. Augustine took over fourteen years to write his response to these criticisms, and in so doing, articulated a political theology of the greatest significance. He argued that the Christian martyrs did not die in order to preserve the inviolability of the state. The earthly city is only a figure, the shadow of the heavenly city which takes shape through history. Human life is a pilgrimage; our citizenship is lodged in the new Jerusalem; our satisfaction is in God alone.

Expounding the Scriptures was the highest priority of Augustine's episcopate. His preferred texts were the Psalms, and the Gospel and First Epistle of John. His *Exposition of the Psalms* collates his meditations on the psalter over a period of at least twenty-four years, from 392 until 416 (or 422). It is an intensely moving collection, and is deeply personal. In addition, over five hundred sermons have survived. They are windows into the world of Late Antiquity through which we glimpse Augustine the pastor responding to the needs of his people in language that was straightforward and direct. His style was lively and warm, his imagery arresting. Of all his works, there is no doubt that his preaching is the most accessible to the modern reader.

'Delight' and 'desire' and 'love' were prominent words in Augustine's spiritual vocabulary. He recognised in these terms essential marks of our humanity. What is it we desire and long for? What is it we want? For Augustine there was only one sufficient answer to these questions: God, who is both source and goal of our desires. His spirituality cuts right across modern preoccupation with self-fulfilment. In company with all the Church Fathers, Augustine taught that it is a fallacy to think that we can find total or final fulfilment of our human and spiritual aspirations in this present life. Human restlessness is endemic. It is a reality not to be ignored, escaped from or anaesthetised, but to be embraced as gift because it projects us into the embrace of the living God in whom alone is rest and peace.

Augustine died in 430 as the barbarians were besieging Hippo. As he lay dying, he instructed that the penitential psalms of David be pinned to the wall beside him that he might die with the prayer on his lips: 'God be merciful to me, a sinner.'

All things change: God alone abides

In one of the psalms it is written, 'You, O Lord, are the same and your years will never end.'[4] My brothers and sisters, do our years never end? They slip away from us day by day. Those years which have been no longer exist; those which lie in the future have yet to be given us. What is past is dead, and what is to come will likewise, in due course, pass into oblivion. Today, my friends, this moment in which we speak, is all that exists. The first hours of today have already passed, the remainder of the day has yet to come; come it will, but only to pass into oblivion . . . Nothing that exists remains constant. Even the human body is subject to a continual process of change; it has no permanence. It ages, it changes with the passage of time and the circumstances of our lives, with disease and accident. It has no constancy. Even the stars have no constancy: they go through patterns of their own, though these changes are not always obvious to us. They move in relation to one another, they whirl through space, moving from east to west, and back again towards the east. They do not rest; they are not the same.

Nor is the human heart any more constant! Consider how many thoughts and distractions assail it. Consider the effect pleasure has upon us, how various cravings can wreak havoc inside us. The human mind is termed rational, but it too changes and possesses no stability. One moment we want something; the next moment we change our mind. One moment we are convinced of something; the next moment we are no longer so sure. One moment we remember; the next moment we forget. No one has an inner coherence of being . . . It is important to allow all this frustration, these diseases, difficulties, troubles and pains, to humble us so that we return to the One who is always the same. And let us enter that city whose inhabitants share in the stability [of God].

Exposition of Psalm 121, 6; (in Hebrew: Psalm 122).

Our heart is restless O God, until it rests in you

'You are great, Lord, and highly to be praised; great is your power and your wisdom is immeasurable.'[5] Man, a little piece of your creation, desires to praise you, a human being 'bearing his mortality with him',[6] carrying with him the witness of his sin and the witness that you 'resist the proud'.[7] Nevertheless, to praise you is the desire of man, a little piece of your creation. You stir man to take pleasure in praising you, because you have made us for yourself, and our heart is restless until it rests in you.

'Grant me, Lord to know and to understand'[8] which comes first – to call upon you or to praise you, and whether knowing you precedes calling upon you. But who calls upon you when he does not know you? For an ignorant person might call upon someone else instead of the right one. But surely, you may be called upon in prayer that you may be known. Yet 'how shall they call upon him in whom they have not believed? and how shall they believe without a preacher?'[9] 'They will praise the Lord who seek for him.'[10]

In seeking him they find him, and in finding they will praise him. Lord, I would seek you, calling upon you – and calling upon you is itself an act of believing in you. You have been preached to us. My faith, Lord, calls upon you. It is your gift to me. You have breathed it into me by the humanity of your Son, by the ministry of your preacher.[11] But how shall I call upon my God, my God and Lord? Surely when I call on him, I am calling on him to come into me. But what place is there in me where my God can enter into me? 'God made heaven and earth.'[12] Lord my God, is there any room in me which can contain you? Can heaven and earth, which you have made and in which you have made me, contain you? Without you, whatever exists would not exist. Then, can what exists contain you? I also have being. So why do I request you to come to me when, unless you were within me, I would have no being at all? . . .

Who then are you, my God? What, I ask, but God who is Lord? For 'who is the Lord but the Lord', or 'who is God but our God?'[13] Most high, utterly good, utterly powerful, most omnipotent, most merciful and most just, deeply hidden and yet most intimately present, perfection of both beauty and strength, stable and incomprehensible, immutable and yet changing all things, never new, never old, ever making everything new and 'leading' the proud 'to be old without their knowledge';[14] always active, always in repose, gathering to yourself but not in need, supporting and filling and protecting, creating and nurturing and bringing to maturity, searching even though to you nothing is lacking: you love without burning, you are jealous in a way that is free from anxiety, you 'repent' without the pain of regret, you are wrathful and remain tranquil. You will a change without any change in your design. You recover what you find, yet have never lost. Never in any need, you rejoice in your gains; you are never avaricious, yet you require interest. We pay you more than you require so as to make you our debtor, yet who has anything that does not belong to you? You pay off debts, though owing nothing to anyone; you cancel debts and incur no loss. But in these words what have I said, my God, my life, my holy sweetness? What has anyone achieved in words when he speaks about you? Yet woe to those who are silent about you because, though loquacious with verbosity, they have nothing to say.

Who will enable me to find rest in you? Who will grant me that you come to my heart and intoxicate it, so that I forget my evils and embrace my one and only good, yourself? What are you to me? Have mercy so that I may find the words. What am I to you that you command me to love you, and that, if I fail to love you, you are angry with me and threaten me with vast miseries? If I do not love you, is that but a little misery? What a wretch I am! In your mercies, Lord God, tell me what you are to me. 'Say to my soul, I am your salvation.'[15] Speak to me so that I may hear. See the ears of my heart are before you, Lord. Open them and 'say to my soul, I am your salvation.' After that utterance I will run and lay hold on you. Do not hide your face from me. Lest I die, let me die so that I may see it.[16] The house of my soul is too small for you to come to it. May it be enlarged by you. It is in ruins: restore it. In your eyes it has offensive features. I admit it, I know it; but who will clean it up? To whom shall I cry other than you?

Confessions, I, i (1) – v (6); ET Henry Chadwick, pp.3-6.

Searching for God in our memories

You are the Lord God of the mind. All things are liable to change. But you remain immutable above all things; and yet have deigned to dwell in my memory since the time that I learnt about you. Why do I ask in which area of my memory you dwell, as if there really are places there? Surely my memory is where you dwell, because I remember you since first I learnt of you, and I find you there when I think about you.

Where then did I find you to be able to learn of you? You were not already in my memory before I learnt of you. Where then did I find you so that I could learn of you if not in the fact that you transcend me? There is no place, whether we go backwards or forwards; there can be no question of place. O truth, everywhere you preside over all who ask counsel of you. You respond at one and the same time to all, even though they are consulting you on different subjects. You reply clearly, but not all hear you clearly. All ask your counsel on what they desire, but do not always hear what they would wish. Your best servant is the person who does not attend so much to hearing what he himself wants, as to willing what he has heard from you.

Late have I loved you, beauty so old and so new; late have I loved you. And see, you were within me and I was in the external world and sought you there, and in my unlovely state I plunged into those lovely created things which you made. You were with me, and I was not with you. The lovely things kept me from you, though if they did not have their existence in you, they would have had no existence at all. You called and cried out loud to me and shattered my deafness. You were radiant and resplendent, you put to flight my blindness. You were fragrant, and I drew in my breath and now pant after you. I tasted you, and now I feel nothing but hunger and thirst for you. You touched me, and I am set on fire to attain the peace which is yours.

When I shall have adhered to you with the whole of myself, I shall never have pain and toil, and my entire life will be full of you. You lift up the person whom you fill. But for the present, because I am not full of you, I am a burden to myself. There is a struggle between joys over which I should be weeping and regrets at matters over which I ought to be rejoicing, and which side has the victory, I do not know. There is a struggle between my regrets at my evil past and my memories of good joys, and which side has the victory, I do not know. Alas, 'Lord, have mercy upon me',[17] wretch that I am. See, I do not hide my wounds. You are the physician, I am the patient. You are pitiful, and I need your pity.

Confessions, X, xxv (36) – xxviii (39); ET Chadwick, pp.201-2.

Our capacity for God

The life of a good Christian is an experience of an ever deepening desire for God. What you desire you cannot, as yet, see; but the desire gives you the capacity, so that when you eventually see you are satisfied. Imagine that you are filling some sort of bag. You know the bulk of what you will be given so you stretch the opening of the sack or the skin or whatever it is to accommodate it. You know how big the object is but you realise that the bag is too small so you increase its capacity by stretching it. In the same way, by deferring our hope, God is stretching our desire, and by deepening our desire he is expanding our soul and increasing its capacity.

Let us desire, my brothers and sisters, for we are to be filled. In the Scriptures we witness the apostle Paul stretching wide his heart to embrace whatever was to come. He says, 'Not that I have already achieved this or am already perfect; my friends, I do not reckon that I have made it my own as yet.' What, then, Paul are you doing in this life if you have not yet made it your own? 'But one thing I do: forgetting what lies behind me and reaching out for that which lies ahead, I press on towards the goal to win the prize which is God's call to the life above in Christ Jesus.'[18] He describes himself as 'reaching out' and 'pressing on'. He felt himself inadequate to embrace 'what eye has not seen nor ear heard, what has not entered into the human heart.'[19] This is the pattern of our life, an experience of being expanded by desire.

But we are expanded by our desire for God only insofar as we have severed our various yearnings of love of this world. I have already said: 'Empty out that which is to be filled.' You are to be filled with goodness; so pour out what is bad in you. Imagine that God wants to fill you with honey. If you are already full of vinegar where is the honey to go? That is why what was in the vessel must not only be poured out, but the container itself be washed, cleansed and scoured. It may be hard work, but it is necessary in order to make it fit to house something else, whatever it may be. Whether we call it honey or gold or wine is immaterial because the reality we are describing cannot be named, and whatever we want to say is summed up in one word: 'God'. And when we have said 'God', what in fact have we said? That one syllable[20] is the distillation of all we hope for. Whatever is in our power to say must in reality be less than God. So, let us stretch ourselves, reaching out to God so that when he comes he may indeed fill us. 'We shall be like him, for we shall see him as he is.'[21]

Commentary on First Epistle of John, IV, 6.

Simplicity in prayer

If we wish to inherit the true blessed life, the Lord who is that true blessed life has taught us to pray. We do not have to pray with a lot of words as if our being heard depended upon the sophistication with which we express ourselves because we are praying to the One who, as the Lord tells us [in the gospels], 'knows what things we need before we even ask.'[22] . . . Nevertheless, God who knows how to give good gifts to his children urges us to 'ask and to seek and to knock.' Why this should be necessary, given that God knows everything before we even ask, might perplex us. But we should understand that our Lord and God wants us to articulate our needs before him not in order to be informed of our wishes (since to him they cannot be hidden), but rather that through the process of our asking desire may deepen in us, and through desire God is able to prepare us to receive the gifts he wishes to bestow. His gifts are very great: our capacity to receive them is small and meagre. That is why it is said to us [in the Scriptures]: 'Open wide your hearts and do not share the lot of unbelievers.'[23] We are being prepared to receive that which is immensely great, that which eye has not seen because it is not colour, that which ear has not heard because it is not sound, that which has entered no human heart because the human heart must itself expand to enter it. We shall receive in proportion to the simplicity of our faith, the firmness of our hope, and the intensity of our desire . . .

At certain times we need consciously to bring our minds back to the business of prayer, and to detach ourselves from other matters and preoccupations which cool our desire [for God]. We need to remind ourselves by the words we pray to focus on what we desire. This we do to prevent what had begun to grow lukewarm from becoming cold, or worse still, from being entirely extinguished. The solution is to fan our desire regularly into flame. This is why when the apostle Paul says: 'Let your requests be made known to God'[24] his words should not be interpreted as though this is how God becomes aware of them. As I have said, God undoubtedly knew them before ever they were uttered. Paul's words should be understood in the sense that it is in the presence of God that we become aware of our inner desires as we wait patiently upon him in prayer, and that it is not appropriate that they should be paraded before other folk in ostentatious worship . . .

We should welcome all opportunities for extended periods of prayer when other duties involving good and necessary activity do not prevent us – although even in the midst of activity, as I have said, we can still pray without ceasing by cherishing our deepest desire. Praying for long periods is not the same thing as praying 'with much speaking'[25] as some people think. To be verbose is one thing; to extend prayer in the warmth of a desire for God is quite different. In the Scriptures we are told that our Lord himself spent a whole night in prayer, and that in his agony he prayed even more fervently. Is he not giving us an example? In time he is the intercessor we need; in eternity he dwells with the Father and is the hearer of our prayer.

Our brothers and sisters in Egypt[26] are said to offer frequent prayers, but these are very brief and are, so to speak, darted forth like arrows lest their vigilant and alert attention which is vital in prayer be weakened or blunted through being over-extended. In this way they too demonstrate that this sort of mental concentration should not be allowed to become exhausted through excess; or on the other hand, if it is sustained should not be suddenly broken off. Far be it from us then, to use 'much speaking' in our prayer; or if concentration be sustained to curtail our prayer. To use a lot of words when we pray is superfluous. But to long for God in prayer, if the desire and concentration persist, is good. It will necessitate beating upon the door of him to whom we are praying by long and deep stirring of the heart. Often prayer consists more in groans than in words, more in tears than in speech. But God collects our tears;[27] our groaning is not hidden from him who created all things by his Word, and who has no need of human words.

Letter 130, viii (15,17); ix (18); x (19,20).
The Lady Proba, to whom Augustine addressed this letter on prayer, was a member of a noble family, the Anicii Probi. She was a consecrated widow and a grandmother.

Discipleship in an unjust world

What troubles you as a Christian is that you see people who lead evil lives prospering, surrounded by an abundance of things. They appear to enjoy good health, they occupy positions of high rank, their entire households seem safe and sound. You observe the happiness of their families, the flatteries of their dependants, their extraordinary influence, their lives unmarred by sadness. You also observe their moral bankruptcy, their unending affluence, and your heart protests that divine judgement does not exist. It would appear that everything is governed by chance, tossed about on the roundabout of fortune. 'For if God took notice of human affairs,' you reason, 'how could that person's wickedness flourish and my own innocence suffer?'

Each disease of the soul has its own remedy in Scripture. The person who thinks such thoughts should drink the antidote contained in the psalm we are pondering ... Apply the lips of your heart by listening and drink the words you hear: 'Do not vie with the wicked or envy those who do wrong; for they will soon fade like the grass and wither like the green herb.'[28]

What seems a long time to you, to God is short. Abandon yourself to God, and it will become short to you as well. These people are of no account; they live only on the surface and strike no deep root. They may be green throughout winter, but when the summer sun begins to scorch, they wither away. Now is the season of winter, and your glory is not as yet apparent. But if your love is deeply rooted then, like trees in the winter once the frosts pass away and the summer comes, which is the Day of Judgement, the green of the grass fades and the glory of the trees becomes be apparent. 'For you have died,' says the apostle – just like trees in winter: they too appear withered and moribund. What hope have we if we are dead inside? But we are not dead inside: our roots go deep, and where our root is there also is our life, for there is our love. As [Paul] states: 'Your life is hidden with Christ in God.'[29] How can a person thus rooted ever wither?

But when will our spring arrive? When our summer? When shall the glory of foliage clothe our nakedness, and a harvest of fruits be our adornment? When shall all this come to pass? Listen to what Paul goes on to say: 'When Christ, who is your life is revealed, then you also will be revealed with him in glory.' And what of this present time? [As I have said:] ' Do not vie with the wicked or envy those who do wrong.' ... These other people have not put their trust in the Lord with the result that their hopes will perish; they will prove fleeting, frail, ephemeral, transitory, vain. But you, [as the psalmist says,] are to 'trust in the Lord and do good.'[30]

First Exposition of Psalm 36, 3; (in Hebrew: Psalm 37).

134

Prayer in times of stress and confusion

You may perhaps ask why the apostle Paul said, 'We do not know how to pray as we ought.'[31] Certainly it is incredible to believe that either he or those to whom he was writing were ignorant of the Lord's Prayer. Paul cannot have written this either rashly or falsely. What then do we suppose was the reasoning behind his statement?

Is it not that the perplexities and troubles of this world are, for the most part, either a remedy for inflated human pride; or a means of testing and exercising our patience which after due probation and discipline reap a rich reward; or a means of eradicating particular sins? The trouble is that we, not knowing what beneficial purpose these difficulties may serve, simply desire to be rid of the stress immediately. Paul reveals to us that he is not exempt from such ignorance either! He hardly knew how to pray as he ought when, to prevent him becoming elated by the greatness of his revelations, he was given a 'thorn in the flesh, a messenger of Satan to harass' him.[32] This caused him to beg the Lord three times to take it away. Surely this was not to know how to pray as he ought? In the end [Paul] heard the Lord's reply as to why the prayer of such a great man as he was not granted: 'My grace is sufficient for you; my power is made perfect in weakness.'

It is exactly the same for us when we are going through stressful periods in our lives. They can both benefit us and damage us with the result that we too do not know how to pray as we ought. And yet because such experiences are hard and painful, and reinforce our sense of weakness, we pray fervently like everyone else to be rid of them. But we owe this much trust to our Lord God that if he does not take them away, we should not imagine that we are being neglected by him. Instead we should patiently endure the evil, and hope that we will come to share in a greater good. In this way God's strength is perfected in our weakness ...

Incidents such as these are recorded [in Scripture] to prevent people from 'thinking too highly of themselves'.[33] Perhaps they have received an answer to an urgent prayer that it would have been better for them not to have received. Alternatively, if their prayer has not been heard, such incidents prevent them from becoming utterly depressed, despairing of the divine mercy towards them. The reality of their situation may have been that what they were asking [of God] would either have been disastrous for them, or else would have resulted in such good fortune that they would have been corrupted and ruined. In these situations we do not know how to pray as we ought.

So if something happens in our life contrary to our prayer, we should bear the disappointment patiently, giving thanks to God in all circumstances, and not have the slightest doubt that it was more appropriate that God's will be done than our own. The mediator gave us this example [in Gethsemane]. When he had said, 'My Father, if it be possible, let this cup pass from me',[34] transforming the human will which was in him by virtue of his incarnation, he immediately added, 'yet not what I want but what you want.' Not without reason are many made righteous by the obedience of this one man.

Letter 130, xiv (25, 26).

Take care what you love

The apostle Paul says that 'love does no wrong to a neighbour; therefore, love is the fulfilling of the law.'[35] [The question I ask is this:] does love give you permission to harm the person you love? Perhaps you merely do no evil, and perhaps no good either. But does not love make you do everything that lies within your power for the object of your love? Is it not love that prays even for our enemies? How can someone fail a friend when they are wishing well to an enemy? If faith is without love, it will also be without works.

In order to keep the achievements of your faith in their true perspective, learn to unite to it hope and charity. But do not become self-conscious about your behaviour: love cannot be idle. What is the driving force in a person, even to do evil, if it is not love? Show me a love that is idle and unproductive! Crime, adultery, corruption, murder, every kind of indulgence, what are these things if not the products of love? So, purify your love. Divert into the garden the water that was running down the gutter. The same ardour that you currently pour out upon the world, pour out instead upon its Creator.

So, am I telling you to give up loving? Not at all! If you love nothing, you will become lazy, dead, lifeless creatures. Love, by all means; but take care what it is you love.

Second Exposition of Psalm 31, 5; (in Hebrew: Psalm 32).

The two great commandments

Always and at all times, reflect [upon the two great commandments] to love God, with all your heart, and with all your soul, and with all your mind; and your neighbour as yourself. Constantly ponder them, meditate upon them and remember them for they must be practised and fulfilled. Note that the love of God comes first in the order of command, but the love of neighbour comes first in the order of action. The person who would teach you this love in two commandments would not commend to you first your neighbour and then God, but first God and then your neighbour. But because you do not as yet see God, by loving your neighbour you will gain sight of God because in so doing you are purifying your eye for the vision of God. John says this plainly: 'Those who do not love a brother or sister whom they have seen, cannot love God whom they have not seen.'[36]

The same is said to you: Love God. So if you say to me: 'Show me the one whom I am to love', what can I reply except what John himself said: 'No one has ever seen God'?[37] But in saying this, do not think that seeing God is altogether impossible for you; for John also states: 'God is love, and those who abide in love are abiding in God.'[38] Love your neighbour, therefore, and discern the source of that love within you; and in so doing, you will see God.

So then, begin by loving your neighbour: 'Share your bread with the hungry, and bring the homeless poor into your own house; when you see the naked, cover them, and do not hide yourself from your own kin.'[39] In doing this what will happen? 'Then shall your light break forth like the dawn.' Your light is your God; to you he is 'morning light', because after the night of this present world he will come to you: God, who neither rises nor sets; God, who always abides.

Remember too what is said by the apostle Paul: 'Bear one another's burdens, and in this way you will fulfil the law of Christ.'[40] The law of Christ is charity; and charity is not fulfilled unless we bear one another's burdens. When you were weak, your neighbour carried you. Now you are strong, carry your neighbour. In so doing, my brothers and sisters, you will make up what is lacking in you. By loving your neighbour and being concerned about your neighbour, you make progress on your journey. And where is that journey bound if not to the Lord God, the God whom it is our duty to love with all our heart, with all our soul, and with all our mind? We may not yet have reached the Lord, but we do have our neighbour with us. So then, support your fellow traveller that you may come to the One with whom you long to dwell.

Commentary on St John's Gospel, XVII, 7-9.

The City of God

I have taken upon myself the task of defending the glorious City of God against those who prefer their own gods to the Founder of that City. I treat of it both as it exists in this world of time, a stranger among the ungodly, living by faith, and as it stands in the security of its everlasting seat. This security it now awaits in steadfast patience, until 'justice returns to judgement';[41] but it is to attain it hereafter in virtue of its ascendancy over its enemies, when the final victory is won and peace established . . .

I know how great is the effort needed to convince the proud of the power and excellence of humility, an excellence which makes it soar above all the summits of this world, which sway in their temporal instability, overtopping them all with an eminence not arrogated by human pride, but granted by divine grace. For the King and Founder of this City which is our subject has revealed in the Scripture of his people this statement of the divine law: 'God resists the proud, but gives grace to the humble.'[42] This is God's prerogative; but man's arrogant spirit in its swelling pride has claimed it as its own . . .

We see that the two cities were created by two kinds of love: the earthly city was created by self-love reaching the point of contempt for God, the Heavenly City by the love of God carried as far as contempt for self. In fact, the earthly city glories in itself, the Heavenly City glories in the Lord.[43] The former looks for the glory from men, the latter finds its highest glory in God, the witness of a good conscience. The earthly lifts up its head in its own glory, the Heavenly City says to its God: 'My glory; you lift up my head.'[44] In the former, the lust for domination lords it over its princes as over the nations it subjugates; in the other both those put in authority and those subject to them serve one another in love, the rulers by their counsel, the subjects by obedience. The one city loves its own strength shown in its powerful leaders; the other says to its God, 'I will love you, my Lord, my strength.'[45]

In the Heavenly City there will be freedom of will . . . There that precept will find fulfilment: 'Be still and know that I am God.'[46] That will truly be the greatest of Sabbaths; a Sabbath that has no evening, the Sabbath that the Lord approved at the beginning of creation . . . There we shall have leisure to be still, and we shall see that he is God . . . It will be an eighth day, as it were, which is to last for ever, a day consecrated by the resurrection of Christ, foreshadowing the eternal rest not only of the spirit but of the body also. There we shall be still and see; we shall see and we shall love; we shall love and we shall praise. Behold what will be, in the end without end!

The City of God, I Preface; XIV, 28; XXII, 30; ET Henry Bettenson, pp.5, 593, 1091.

To delight in God

Jesus said, 'No one can come to me unless drawn by the Father who sent me.'[47] Do not imagine that you are being drawn [to God] against your will, for the mind can also be drawn by love. Nor should we be afraid of being criticised by those who interpret the words [of Scripture] too literally and are quite incapable of grasping the divine truths they contain. Such folk might object to these words saying: 'How can I believe of my own free will if I am being drawn?' In reply to which I say this: 'You are being drawn not merely by your free will, but also by delight.'

But what does it mean to be drawn by delight? [In the psalms it is written:] 'Let the Lord be your delight, and he will grant you the desires of your heart.'[48] ... And one of our own poets has also said: 'Everyone is drawn by his own dear delight' – note: not by necessity but by delight, not by compulsion but by pleasure. So there is all the more reason to suppose that when people delight in truth, in all that is worthwhile, in righteousness, in the prospect of eternal life, they are in fact being drawn by Christ himself, for Christ is all these things. Or must we assume that although the bodily senses have their delights the mind is not permitted any? If the soul has no delights, how is it that Scripture says: 'All people will take refuge in the shadow of your wings. They will feast on the abundance of your house, and you will give them drink from the river of your delights. For with you is the fountain of life: in your light we see light'?[49]

Show me a lover for lovers understand what I am talking about. Show me someone who wants something, someone who is hungry, someone who is a pilgrim in this wilderness, thirsting and panting for the fountains of their eternal home, show me such a person and he or she will understand what I am saying. But if I am speaking to those without feeling, then they will not know what I am talking about. Offer a handful of green grass to a sheep and you draw it toward you. Show a boy some nuts and he is enticed. The child is drawn by the things he wants to grasp, drawn because he wants them, drawn without physical coercion, drawn simply by the pull of his own appetite. If then, the things that lovers see as the delights and pleasures of the earth can draw them (because it is true that 'everyone is drawn by his own dear delight') then does not Christ draw us when he is revealed to us by the Father? What does the mind desire more strongly than truth? For what does it have an insatiable appetite, and why is it so concerned to cleanse its palate for discerning the truth, unless it is that it may eat and drink wisdom, righteousness, truth and eternity?

In this life we do indeed hunger; but our hopes are fixed on the hereafter when we shall be satisfied. In the gospels Christ speaks both of our present

140

140

experience when he says: 'Blessed are they who hunger and thirst for righteousness', and also of our future hope 'for they shall be satisfied'.[50] And we should also note that when he said, 'No one comes to me unless drawn by the Father who sent me,' he immediately added: 'And I shall raise them up on the last day.' I will give them the thing they love. I will give them all that they hope for. They will behold what they believe but do not as yet see. They will eat what they hunger for and be filled with that for which they thirst. When? At the resurrection of the dead, because 'I will raise them up on the last day.'

Commentary on St John's Gospel, XXVI, 4-6.

The miracle of daily life

The miracle wrought by our Lord Jesus Christ [at Cana in Galilee] in which he turned water into wine, is not marvellous to those who know that God did it. For he who made wine that day at the marriage feast in the six stone water jars which he had ordered to be filled to the brim with water, performs the same miracle each year in vines. Just as what the servants had put into the water jars was changed into wine by the agency of the Lord, so what the clouds pour forth is changed into wine by the agency of the same Lord. We do not marvel at this, simply because it happens each year; familiarity has dulled our capacity for wonder. But it should demand of us a more profound consideration than something which once happened in some water jars. Is there anyone who, contemplating the works of God by which the entire universe is governed and ordered, is not amazed and overwhelmed by a sense of the miraculous? The power and strength of a single grain of seed is itself an amazing thing, inspiring awe in its contemplation. But humanity, preoccupied with its own petty agenda, has lost the capacity to contemplate the works of God by which it should daily render praise to God as Creator.

This is why God has, as it were, reserved to himself certain extraordinary and unexpected actions, in order that by such marvels he might startle people out of their lethargy into worship. A dead man rose again; people marvelled. By contrast, numerous babies are born every day, and no one marvels. If only we would reflect upon life more carefully, we would come to see that it is a greater miracle for a child to be given existence who before did not exist, than for a man to come back to life who already existed . . . People hold cheap what they see every day of their lives, but suddenly, when confronted by extraordinary events, they are dumbfounded, though such events are truly no more wonderful than the others. Governing the universe, for example, is a greater miracle than feeding five thousand people with five loaves of bread, but no one marvels at it. People marvel at the feeding of the five thousand not because this miracle is greater, but because it is out of the ordinary. Who is even now providing nourishment for the whole world if not the God who creates a field of wheat from a few seeds? . . .

Miracles are presented to our senses in order to stimulate our minds. They are put before our eyes in order to engage our understanding, and so make us marvel at the God we do not see through his works which we do see. For then, when we have been raised to the level of faith and purified by faith, we desire to behold, though not with our eyes, the unseen God whom we have recognised through what is seen.

Commentary on St John's Gospel, VIII, 1; XXIV, 1.

Embrace the love of God, and by love embrace God

No one should say: 'I do not know what I love.' If people love their brothers and sisters, then they will love the love that is God. For we know the love with which we love better than the brother or sister who is the object of our love. Thus we can already know God better than we know our brother or sister. We can know God more clearly because he is more clearly present, more deeply within us and therefore more sure. Embrace the love of God, and by love embrace God. Love itself brings together into a common bond of holiness all good angels and all servants of God, and joins us to them and to each other and all of us to God.

In proportion, then, as our inflated egos are healed of their pride, we become more full of love. And with what is a person full who is full of love, if not with God? But you will say: 'I can see love, and as far as I am able, I can conceive of it in my mind; I believe the Scripture when it says that "God is love; and those who abide in love abide in God, and God abides in them";[51] but when I see that, I still do not see the Trinity.' My point is precisely that: you do see the Trinity if you see love . . .

We begin with that which is nearest to us, namely, our brother or sister. Observe how highly the apostle John commends mutual love: 'Whoever loves a brother or sister lives in the light, and in such a person there is no cause for stumbling.'[52] It is manifestly clear that John makes the perfection of righteousness consist in the love of our brothers and sisters; for a person is certainly perfect in whom there is no occasion for stumbling. And yet the apostle seems to have passed over the love of God in silence, something he would never have done if he had not intended God to be understood in the mutuality of love itself. Indeed, in the same epistle he says: 'Beloved, let us love one another because love is from God; everyone who loves is born of God and knows God.'[53] This passage declares succinctly and plainly that such mutuality of love . . . is not only from God, but also is God.

When, therefore, we love our brothers and sisters out of love, we are loving our brothers and sisters out of God. Such love should claim our priority. Moreover, the two commandments cannot exist without each other. Since God is love, a person who loves love, is certainly loving God; and we must needs love love if we are to love our brothers and sisters truly. Hence a little later, [John] says: 'Those who do not love the brother or sister whom they have seen, cannot love God whom they have not seen.'[54] In other words, the reason why a person cannot see God is because he does not love his brothers and sisters . . . So let us stop worrying about how much love we ought to spend on our neighbour and how much on God. The answer is incomparably more on God than on ourselves, and on our sisters and brothers as much as on ourselves. But in reality the more we love God, the more we love ourselves. So, then, we love God and our neighbour out of one and the same love; but we love God for the sake of God, and ourselves and our neighbours for the sake of God.

On the Trinity, VIII, viii (12).

On penitence

We cannot just assume that we are living good lives, free from sin. Let a person's life be praised insofar as that person asks for pardon. As for people without hope, the less attentive they are to their own sins, the more they pry into those of other people. They are seeking not what they can correct, but what they can criticise. And as they are not able to excuse themselves, they are ready to accuse other people. This was not the way that David showed us how to pray and make reparation to God. [In the psalms] he says: 'I acknowledge my transgressions, and my sin is ever before me.'[55] David was not interested in other people's sins. He turned his mind to himself, not in self-flattery, but in entering deeply within himself. He did not spare himself, and thus it was not presumptuous of him to pray that he might be spared.

Do you want to be reconciled to God? Then learn how to act towards yourself that God may be reconciled with you. Notice what you read in the same psalm: 'If you wanted sacrifice, I would give it; but you take no pleasure in burnt offerings.'[56] Will then you have no sacrifice at all? Have you nothing to offer, nothing to appease God at all? ... Go on with the psalm, listen and say: 'The sacrifice of God is a broken spirit: a broken and contrite heart, O God, you will not despise.'[57] You have that to offer. Do not examine the flock. Do not prepare ships and journey to the most distant provinces to bring back perfumes. Seek rather, in your heart what is acceptable to God: you must rend your heart. Why do you fear that it may perish if it is broken? Attend to the words of Scripture: 'Create in me a clean heart, O God.'[58] So then, that a pure heart may be created, let the impure one be broken.

Sermon 19, 2-3.

The mystery of the incarnation

With what words shall we praise the love of God? What thanks shall we give?

God so loved us that for our sakes he, through whom time was made, was made in time; older by eternity than the world itself, he became younger in age than many of his servants in the world; God, who made man, was made man; he was given existence by a mother whom he brought into existence; he was carried in hands which he formed; he nursed at breasts which he filled; he cried like a babe in the manger in speechless infancy – this Word without which human eloquence is speechless!

Sermon 188, 2; (also listed as *On the Seasons*, 25; and *On Christmas* 6); ET Thomas Lawler, ACW, 15, Newman Press/ Paulist Press, New York, 1952, p.93.

Praying for Christian unity

My brothers and sisters, I beg you above all else to show charity not only towards one another, but also to those who are outside our communion whether they be pagans who do not know Christ, or Christians separated from us,[59] those who profess their faith in the head [Jesus Christ] while separated from the body. Let us grieve for them, my friends, as though they were our own brothers and sisters. For they are our brothers and sisters whether they like it or not. They will only cease to be our brothers and sisters when they cease to say 'Our Father' . . .

They may say: 'Why do you seek us out? Why do you want us?' And we will answer: 'Because you are our brothers and sisters.' They may say: 'Go away! We have nothing in common with you!' But we shall reply that we absolutely do have something in common: we profess one Christ; thus we ought to be united in one body under one head.

I therefore beg you, my brothers and sisters, through the very depth of that love by whose milk we are nourished and by whose bread we are fortified; I beg you through our Lord Jesus Christ and his gentleness. It is now time that we show them great charity and overflowing mercy in praying to God for them that God may finally bring them to their senses, so that they turn and see that they have nothing at all to say against the truth. Nothing is left to them except the weakness of animosity which is all the weaker the more strength it claims for itself. I beg you on behalf of the weak, on behalf of those who reason according to this world, on behalf of those who are crude and carnal, on behalf of those who are nevertheless our brothers and sisters. They celebrate the same sacraments even though they do not celebrate them together with us. They respond with the same 'Amen' which, even though they do not say it together with us, yet it is the same. So pour out the depth of your love to God on their behalf.

Second Exposition of Psalm 32, 29; (in Hebrew: Psalm 33).

Be yourselves the praise you speak

In the psalms it says, 'O sing to the Lord a new song; sing his praise in the assembly of the saints.'[60] We are urged to sing to the Lord a new song. It is a new person who knows a new song. A song is a joyful thing, and if we reflect more deeply, it is also a matter of love. Thus anyone who has learned how to love a new life will also have learned how to sing a new song. For the sake of the new song, however, we need to be reminded what the nature of the new life is. Indeed a new person, a new song and the new covenant are all manifestations of the one kingdom: a new person will both sing a new song and belong to the new covenant.

Everybody loves; the question is, what is the object of their love? [In Scripture] we are not urged not to love, but instead to choose what we love. But how can we choose unless we are first chosen? We cannot even love unless we are first loved. Listen to the words of John the apostle: 'We love because God first loved us.'[61] If you investigate why it is that people love God, you will discover absolutely no other reason than that God loved them. God has given us himself: God is both the object of our love and the source of our love. And if you want to know what has been given us as the source of our love, you will find a clearer explanation in the words of the apostle Paul: 'The love of God has been poured into our hearts.'[62] Where does it come from? From ourselves? No. Then from where? 'Through the Holy Spirit who has been given to us.' With this assurance, then, let us love God by the gift of God . . . God offers himself to us;[63] there is no need to offer us more. He calls out to us: 'Love me and you will possess me, because you cannot love me unless you possess me.'

My brothers and sisters, my children, infants of the Catholic Church, O holy and heavenly seed, you who have been born again in Christ, born from above, listen to me – or rather, listen to God through me: 'Sing to the Lord a new song.' 'But I do sing', you reply. Yes, you do sing; of course you sing. I can hear you! But make sure that your life is singing the same tune as your tongue. Sing with your voices, sing with your hearts, sing with your lips, sing with your lives . . . And if you ask me what you should sing in praise of God, and you are busy looking for songs, then know that the singer himself is the praise contained in the song. Do you want to speak the praise of God? Then be yourselves what you speak. If you lead good lives, you are God's praise.

Sermon 34, 1-3, 5-6.

The strength of knowing your weakness

Some people's strength is based not on wealth, or in a sense of their physical well-being, or even in the power that their position in society afford them, but in a sense of their own righteousness. Above all others, it is these people whom we should guard ourselves against. They should be feared and repulsed, and in no way imitated. As I say, the individuals who concern me are not so much those who rely on their physical prowess, or private means, their class or status – things which are temporal, fleeting, unreliable, and ephemeral – but rather those with an in-built confidence in their own righteousness.

It was precisely this kind of strength that prevented the Jewish leaders from passing through the eye of the needle. They took their righteousness for granted, and in their own eyes considered themselves healthy. They had no need of medicine, and the physician himself they slew. They were strong; they were not weak! And that is why they did not respond to the call of the One who said, 'It is not the healthy who need a doctor but the sick. I have come to call not the righteous, but sinners to repentance.'[70] The people who ridiculed Christ's disciples because their master visited the homes of the sick and dared to eat with them were the strong ones. 'Why,' they said, 'does your master eat with tax collectors and sinners?'[71] O you strong ones who boast that you have no need of a doctor! This strength of yours is not healthy; it is born of madness! Nothing is stronger than a madman; a madman can intimidate even the strongest of men. So although these people appear strong to the rest of us, in fact they are teetering on the edge of their own self-destruction. God grant that we may never imitate such strength.

We should dread the possibility that anyone should want to imitate such people. The teacher of humility, who shared our weakness and deigned to give us a share in his divinity, came to teach us the way; indeed, to be the Way himself. It was his own humility that he impressed upon us. He even willingly submitted to be baptised by one of his own servants, so that we might learn to confess our sins and know our own weakness, because only in so doing can we become truly strong. As Paul the Apostle was to say, 'When I am weak, then I am strong.'[72]

Christ rejected the path of strength. But these people, who crave to be strong in life and end up relying on their own virtue as their self-justification, all they succeed in doing is tripping over the stumbling block.[73] In their eyes, the Lamb was a goat, and because they did not recognise him as such, they killed him. They were not worthy to be redeemed by the Lamb. In their strength they attacked Christ, priding themselves in their own sense of justice. Just listen to those ones talking. They had sent certain individuals from Jerusalem to arrest Christ, but when it came to it, they did not do so. 'Why did you not seize him?' they asked.[74] 'No one ever spoke like this man,' was the reply to which the strong ones retorted, 'Have you seen any of the Pharisees believing in him? Or any of the scribes? It is only people ignorant of the law who believe in him.'

In this way they put themselves a cut above the sick multitude who ran to the doctor. Why did they exalt themselves? Because they thought of themselves as strong. And what is worse, by their strength they managed to entice the multitude into their camp, and ended up killing the physician who had power to heal them all. But the murdered physician, by his very death, compounded a medicine out of his own blood to heal the sick.

First Exposition of Psalm 58, 7; (in Hebrew: Psalm 59)

God is your peace, your life and your eternity

In the psalms, David says, 'The meek shall inherit the land and delight in an abundance of peace.'[64] Let the wicked find their delight in an abundance of gold and silver, in an abundance of slaves, palm groves, rose trees and choice wines, in splendid and sumptuous banquets. Is this the power you covet? Is this the flower that delights you? Even if it were to last for ever, would it not in the end be a matter for tears?

But what are your delights to be? Listen again to the words [of the psalmist]: and they shall 'delight in an abundance of peace'. Peace – that is your gold and your silver; peace is your prosperity; peace is your life; and peace is your God. Peace will fulfil your every desire. In this life gold cannot become your silver; what is wine cannot become your bread; your light cannot become your drink as well. But your God will be everything to you: God will be your meat so that you no longer hunger; your drink so that you no longer thirst; your enlightening so that you do not stumble. God, whole and entire, will possess you whole and entire. You will not feel cramped for space in possessing God with whom you possess everything. In his embrace you shall have all and God shall have all, because you and God will be one.

First Exposition of Psalm 36, 12; (in Hebrew: Psalm 37).

We are an Easter people and 'Alleluia' is our song

Let us sing 'Alleluia' here and now in this life, even though we are oppressed by various worries, so that we may sing it one day in the world to come when we are set free from all anxiety. Why is it that we worry so much in this life? It is hardly surprising that I should worry when I read [in the Scriptures]: 'Are not the days of our life full of trouble?'[65] Are you surprised that I am worried when I hear the words: 'Watch and pray that you enter not into temptation'?[66] Are you surprised that I am worried when in the face of so many temptations and troubles the Lord's Prayer orders us to pray: 'Forgive us our debts as we also forgive our debtors'?[67] Every day we pray and every day we sin. Do you think that I can be free from anxiety when every day I need to seek pardon for my sins and help in the face of difficulties? When I have said for my past sins: 'Forgive us our debts as we also forgive our debtors,' I immediately go on to add, because of the difficulties that lie ahead: 'Lead us not into temptation.' How can the congregation be in security when it cries out with me: 'Deliver us from evil'? And yet, my brothers and sisters, in this evil plight of ours we must nevertheless sing 'Alleluia' to the good God who delivers us from evil.

In the middle of the dangers and trials that beset us we and all people must sing 'Alleluia', for as Paul says, 'God is faithful and God will not let you be tempted beyond your strength.'[68] So then, we too must sing 'Alleluia'. Men and women may be sinful, but God is faithful. And note, Scripture does not say, 'God will not let you be tempted,' but rather 'God will not let you be tempted beyond your strength, but with the temptation God will also provide a means of escape that you may be able to endure it.' If you enter temptation God will also provide a means of escape so that you do not perish in temptation. Just as a potter forms a vase, so you are to be moulded by preaching; you are to be fired in the kiln of tribulation. Thus when you enter temptation, think of a means of escape; for God is faithful. [As one of the Psalms has it:] 'The Lord will preserve your coming in and your going out.'[69] . . .

How happy will be our shout of 'Alleluia' [as we enter heaven], how carefree, how secure from any assault, where no enemy lurks and no friend dies. There praise is offered to God, and here also, but here it is offered by anxious people and there by those who are free from all anxiety; here by those who must die, there by those who will live for ever. Here praise is offered in hope, there by those who enjoy the reality; here by pilgrims in transit, there by those who have reached their homeland.

So my friends, let us sing 'Alleluia', albeit not in the enjoyment of the heavenly rest, but in order to sweeten our toil in this life. Let us sing as travellers sing on a journey; but keep on walking. Lighten your toil by singing and never be idle. Sing but keep on walking. And what do I mean by walking? I mean press on from good to better. The apostle says that there are some who go from bad to worse, but if you persevere, you will keep on walking. Advance in virtue, in true faith and in right conduct. Sing up – and keep on walking!

Sermon 256, 1.

NOTES

1 Manichaeism takes its name from a Persian called Mani who lived in the second century. It was gnostic in origin, conscious of having 'unveiled' truths of universal validity. It professed a radical dualism in which the principle of light was opposed by the evil principle in an eternal struggle. It boasted an elaborate doctrinal system and severe moral asceticism. According to Augustine, however, evil is not a substance but a lack of good. Its presence in the world is the fault of man who freely rebelled against God. Against the Manichees, he also upheld the authority and unity of both Old and New Testaments.

2 The Donatist Schism dated from the time of the persecution under Diocletian. The election of Cecilian as primate of Carthage had been contested by the Numidian bishops who offered a rival candidate. He was succeeded by Donatus who gave his name to the schism. They took a decisive stand against the readmission to communion of bishops who had handed over sacred books to the authorities during the persecution. In their view they had forfeited their right and capacity to preside over the Church. According to the Donatists, the Church was a society of saints, the elect of God. Sacraments (including that of Holy Orders) administered by unworthy clergy were invalid.

   Against the Donatists, Augustine preached the primacy of love. He argued that it is Christ who baptises, ordains, consecrates, not Peter or Augustine or Judas. If the grace of God is operative in the sacraments, the worthiness of the minister (or lack of it) is irrelevant. Furthermore the Church is a mixed body of saints and sinners, and the separation of the two is God's business not man's.

3 Aspects of Augustine's teaching, particularly the linkage of the concept of original sin to sexual intercourse which contributed to the formation of such a negative attitude to sexuality in the West, remain controversial.

4 Psalm 102: 27.
5 Psalm 48: 2; Psalm 147: 5.
6 2 Corinthians 4: 10.
7 1 Peter 5: 5.
8 Psalm 119: 34.
9 Romans 10: 14.
10 Psalm 22: 27.
11 Augustine is probably referring to Ambrose rather than to Christ (cf., *Letter* 147).
12 Genesis 1: 1.
13 Psalm 18: 32.
14 Job 9: 5, Old Latin version.
15 Psalm 35: 3.
16 *Moriar ne moriar, ut eam videam.* No one can see the face of God and live (Exodus 33: 20); yet in the vision of God consists man's life and joy.
17 Psalm 31: 10.
18 Philippians 4: 12-14.
19 1 Corinthians 2: 9.
20 literally 'two syllables' – *Deus*.
21 1 John 3: 2.
22 Matthew 6: 8.
23 2 Corinthians 6: 13, 14.
24 Philippians 4: 6.
25 Matthew 6: 7.

26 Augustine is probably referring to the monks of Egypt and their style of prayer, rather than to Scripture and the Israelites in Egypt.
27 Psalm 56: 8.
28 Psalm 37: 1.
29 Colossians 3: 3.
30 Psalm 37: 3.
31 Romans 8: 26.
32 2 Corinthians 12: 7.
33 Romans 12: 3.
34 Matthew 26: 39; Mark 14: 36; Luke 22: 42.
35 Romans 13: 10.
36 1 John 4: 20.
37 1 John 4: 12.
38 1 John 4: 16.
39 Isaiah 58: 7, 8.
40 Galatians 6: 2.
41 Psalm 94: 15.
42 James 4: 6.
43 2 Corinthians 10: 17.
44 Psalm 3: 3.
45 Psalm 18: 1.
46 Psalm 46: 10.
47 John 6: 44.
48 Psalm 37: 4.
49 Psalm 36: 7-9.
50 Matthew 5: 6.
51 1 John 4: 16.
52 1 John 2: 10.
53 1 John 4: 7.
54 1 John 4: 20.
55 Psalm 51: 3.
56 Psalm 51: 16.
57 Psalm 51: 17.
58 Psalm 51: 10.
59 Augustine is referring here to the Donatists; see above n.2.
60 Psalm 96: 1, 3.
61 1 John 4: 10.
62 Romans 5: 5.
63 *in compendio* – literally 'at bargain price'. The image is commercial. God is offering himself at no price at all; indeed, at a profit to us. i.e. the opposite of *dispendium* or 'expense'.
64 Psalm 37: 11.
65 Psalm 90: 10.
66 Matthew 26: 41; Mark 14: 38.
67 Matthew 6: 12.
68 1 Corinthians 10: 13.
69 Psalm 121: 8.
70 Matthew 9: 12, 13.
71 Matthew 9: 11.

72 2 Corinthians 12: 10.
73 Romans 9: 32.
74 John 7: 45.

SELECT BIBLIOGRAPHY

Augustine's literary output was prodigious and it is impossible to reproduce here a suitable bibliography.

<u>TEXTS and TRANSLATIONS</u>
PL 32-46.
The principal works have modern critical editions of the Teubner text in CCSL and CSEL. Not all of his works are in English translation, but there are numerous translations of his principal works, some modern, others rather dated now. *The Works of St Augustine: A Translation for the 21st Century*, New City, New York, 1990- , is in preparation, parts of which are already available.

a) Confessions
ET Henry Chadwick, OUP, New York and Oxford, 1991.

b) The City of God
ET Henry Bettenson with introduction by David Knowles, Penguin, Baltimore and
    Harmondsworth, 1972.

c) On the Trinity
The Later Works, selected and ET John Burnaby, LCC, 1955.

d) Sermons
The Works of St Augustine: A Translation for the 21st Century, Part III: Sermons, ET
    with notes Edmund Hill, New City, New York, 1990- .
Selected sermons also in ACW (various volumes).

e) Letters
NPNF 1.

f) Exposition of the Book of Psalms
NPNF 8.
St Augustine on the Psalms, ACW 29, selected and ET Scholastica Hebgin and
    Felicitas Corrigan, 1960.
The Still Waters of Beauty, selected and ET Adrian Roberts and Oliver Davies, with
    introduction by Angela Ashwin, New City, London, Dublin, Edinburgh, 1993.

<u>STUDIES and ARTICLES</u>
Bonner, Gerald, *Augustine: Life and Controversies*, Canterbury Press, Norwich, 1986.
Bonner, Gerald, 'Augustine of Hippo', *Dictionary of Christian Spirituality*, SCM,
    London, 1983, pp.33-5.
Brown, Peter, *Augustine of Hippo*, Faber, London, 1967 and reprints; University of
    California Press, Berkeley, 1969 and reprints; excellent and engaging.
Burnaby, John, *Amor Dei*, Hodder and Stoughton, London, 1938 and reprints; still the
    greatest intellectual biography.
Chadwick, Henry, *St Augustine*, OUP, 1986 (Past Masters Series).
Clark, Mary T., *Augustine*, Geoffrey Chapman, London, 1994 (Outstanding Christian
    Thinkers Series).
Evans, G.R., *Augustine on Evil*, CUP, 1982.
Van der Meer, F., (ET) *Augustine the Bishop*, London, 1961.

7

Benedict
SEEKING GOD

'Prefer nothing to the love of Christ.'
RULE OF ST BENEDICT

'Some years ago there lived a man called Benedict, who was revered for the holiness of his life. Indeed, he was blessed by God not only in name, but also in nature.'[1] With these words, Gregory the Great introduces the subject of the second book of his *Dialogues*. Written some forty years after Benedict's death, and based on the memories of actual witnesses, the book constitutes the main source of information about Benedict. From it we learn that he was born in about 480 in Nursia, a little town roughly seventy miles north-east of Rome. The world into which he was born was unstable, and the changes that were occurring were not dissimilar to what has been observed in recent years following the collapse of the Soviet Union. In 476 the last Western emperor had been deposed; civic life was at a low ebb; the empire was disintegrating, and there was a steady drift of population away from the cities into rural areas, seeking the protection of rich and powerful landed families.

At the age of twenty Benedict was sent to study in Rome but, appalled at the decadent culture around him, withdrew to live as a hermit for three years in a cave at Subiaco, about thirty miles outside Rome. His manner of life attracted disciples and he established a number of monasteries in the locality, each with an abbot. He directed these monasteries for about twenty-five years until sadly, jealousy and intrigue forced him and the small band of monks loyal to him to move to Monte Cassino. There he spent the remaining seventeen years or so of his life establishing a monastery and converting a formerly pagan area to Christianity. He died on 21 March in about 547.

Towards the end of his life, Benedict distilled his experience of monastic life into what he called 'a little *Rule* for beginners.'[2] It is this document that had a profound impact upon the shape of Western spirituality. As Pope Gregory commented: 'Benedict wrote a *Rule* for monks that is remarkable for its discretion and its clarity of language. Anyone who wants to know more about his life and character can discover his portrait in his *Rule*, since his life cannot have differed from his teaching.'[3] In the centuries that followed, monasteries proliferated. They emerged as strong communities of prayer and learning; places of hospitality in a violent age that spoke to a fragile, frightened world of the stability and faithfulness of God.

For all Pope Gregory's praise, many people today, perhaps because they expect a learned or mystical document, find Benedict's *Rule* disappointing. Its concepts are simple, its language is unpretentious. There is little at first glance that seems 'relevant'. Reflection, however, reveals just how topical many of the issues that Benedict dealt with are. Prayer, stewardship of resources, personal relationships, obedience, community living, work, lifestyle, coping with injustice and disappointment, are significant matters for a Christian in every age. Benedict was not concerned with articulating a spiritual theory for the pious, but with conversion of the heart, with forming attitudes in people, and rooting prayer in the ordinariness of daily life.

The main source for Benedict's *Rule* was Scripture from which he quoted lavishly. Indeed the *Rule* was essentially an application of the Gospel to life lived in community. He drew upon earlier monastic documents, including the teaching of Basil, John Cassian, and a slightly earlier, anonymous monastic text called *The Rule of the Master*. The merit of Benedict's *Rule*, however, was that it was short, clear, and moderate. He even advocated a measure of discretion and flexibility. He did not write an ideal *Rule* for ideal monks: he wrote conscious of his own frailty, anticipating that his monks would fail because they, like him, were sinners in need of God's grace and forgiveness. Perhaps this is why Benedict's *Rule* has endured, and why it continues to appeal to such a wide public.

In the *Rule*, the call to prayer had the first claim upon the time and energy of both individual and community: 'Let nothing be preferred to the work of God.'[4] Benedict's words resonate with the language of John's gospel,[5] and underscore an understanding of prayer as God's activity: healing, setting free, making people whole and holy. Benedict stood within an inheritance of liturgical prayer: he received a tradition, and adapted and reformed it to meet the needs of his own day. He commended a framework and rhythm of prayer with seven offices during the day and vigils at night. It was a way of sanctifying time. The Office (Opus Dei) was praise-centred and consisted in the recitation of all one hundred and fifty psalms on a seven-day cycle, of readings from Scripture and recognised orthodox commentaries, and prayers. Benedict hardly ever referred to the Eucharist, and it is probable that the Eucharist was celebrated in his monasteries only on Sundays and feast days. It is worth noting that Benedict himself was never ordained. Monastic spirituality was oriented to the Office, not the Eucharist. *Lectio divina*, the prayerful reading of Scripture, complemented communal prayer, and also occupied a significant amount of a monk's time. It enabled a monk to internalise the Scriptures so that they began to form a reservoir of spiritual wisdom from which to sustain prayer at all times and occasions. To seek God and to delight in his will was the hallmark of Benedict's spirituality.

Benedict accorded the utmost importance to the character and ministry of the abbot. The abbot was elected by the community for life and fulfilled many roles. He was administrator and spiritual director. Above all, he was the recipient of the obedience of those who had heard the call to follow the monastic path because he was 'believed to hold the place of Christ in the monastery.'[6] It was a matter of faith. Benedict's words contrast with our modern suspicion of authority in general, and our tendency to view obedience at best as repressive, and at worst as spiritual tyranny in disguise. For Benedict, however, the root of obedience lay in listening.[7] The opening words of the prologue – 'Listen carefully, my son,' are indicative of the whole tone of the *Rule*: the monastic life was about listening to God in community, and therefore about relationship and trust. This explains why on the one hand, silence was so highly prized, and on the other hand, why one of the worst sins for Benedict was that of 'murmuring'.

The monk lived out his baptism in a life committed to stability in community, conversion to the monastic way of life (*conversatio morum*), and obedience. In other words, the monk gave himself to God in a particular place, with particular companions, with this particular work to do. As in the desert monasticism of Egypt, Benedict expected his monks to 'live by the labour of their hands'.[8] They were to be self-supporting, but they worked for the same reason they engaged in study and liturgical prayer – as a means of truly seeking God. To this end, Benedict advocated a balanced life. The monk was to labour without being dehumanised, and to rest without frittering life away in idleness or gossip.

For Benedict, the whole of life was spiritual. Even the tools of the monastery were to be reverenced in the same way as the vessels of the altar.[9] God was everywhere and to be encountered at all times and in every human being. Christ was to be met not only in the abbot, but also in the sick, the guest, and in one's brother. Benedict had a fundamentally incarnational view of life. As Pope Gregory commented in the extract from the *Dialogues* that concludes this section, Benedict saw the whole world in God, permeated by divine light.

Listening to God in community

Listen carefully, my son, to the instructions of your teacher, and attend with the ear of your heart to the advice of a loving father. Welcome it, and faithfully put it into practice; so that through the labour of obedience you may return to the God from whom you have drifted through the sloth of disobedience. To you, then, whomever you may be, are my words addressed, that renouncing your own will, and taking up the strong and glorious weapons of obedience, you may do battle in the service of Christ the Lord, our true King.

First of all, whenever you begin a good work, you must pray to God most urgently to bring it to perfection, so that he who has delighted to count us among his children, may never be saddened by our evil lives. For we must always serve God with the gifts he has given us that he may never as an angry parent disinherit us or like some dreaded master, enraged by our sins, hand us over to eternal punishment as worthless servants who have refused to follow him in the way to glory.

Let us then at last arouse ouselves! For the Scriptures challenge us to do so in these words: 'Now is the time for us to rise from sleep.'[10] Let us open wide our eyes to the light that transfigures, and unstop our ears to the thunder of God's voice which daily cries out to us: 'O that today you would listen to his voice and harden not your hearts![11] And again [Scripture says]: 'You that have ears to hear, listen to what the Spirit is saying to the churches!'[12] And what is the Spirit saying? 'Come, my children, listen to me and I will teach you the fear of the Lord.' 'Run while you have the light of life, lest the darkness of death overtake you.'[13]

Moreover the Lord, searching among the crowds for labourers, calls out again in these words: 'Is there anyone here who desires life and is eager to see good days?'[14] And if, hearing his voice, you reply, 'I do,' then God says to you: '"If you want to have true and eternal life, keep your tongue from vicious talk and your lips from uttering lies. Turn from evil and do good; seek peace and pursue it."[15] For when you do this, my eyes will rest upon you and my ears will be open to your prayers, and before you call to me, I shall say to you: "Here I am."'[16]

Dear friends, what can be more delightful than this voice of the Lord inviting us? Behold, in his loving mercy, the Lord is showing us the way of life. Clothed then with faith and the performance of good works, and with the Gospel as our guide, let us set out on this way of life that we may deserve to see the God 'who is calling us to share in his kingdom.'[17]

The Rule of St Benedict, prologue.

Let us hasten to do now what will profit us for eternity

The Lord says in the Gospel, 'Everyone who hears these words of mine and acts upon them, is like a sensible man who built his house on rock; the floods came, the winds blew and beat upon the house but it did not fall because it was founded upon rock.'[18] Having given us these instructions, the Lord expects us each day to respond and to translate his holy teaching into action. In order that we may make amends for our evil ways, the Lord lengthens the days of our life by way of a truce. As the apostle Paul says: 'Do you not realise that the patience of God is meant to invite you to repentance?'[19] Indeed, the merciful Lord assures us: 'I do not desire the death of sinners but rather that they should turn from their wickedness and live.'[20]

My friends, we have asked the Lord about the kind of person who dwells in his tabernacle, and we have heard what is required in order to do so. All that remains for us is to fulfil this duty. This means that our hearts and bodies must be prepared to engage in the warfare of holy obedience to God's commands. So let us ask God that he be pleased, where our nature is powerless, to give us the help of his grace. And, if we wish to escape the punishment of hell and reach eternal life, then while there is still time, while we are in this body and can accomplish all these things by the light of life, let us hasten to do now what will profit us for eternity.

We propose, therefore, to establish a school of the Lord's service.[21] In founding this we hope that we shall not make rules that are harsh or burdensome. But if, for the good of all concerned, for the correction of faults or the preservation of charity, there be some strictness of discipline, do not be immediately daunted and run away from the way that leads to salvation. Its entrance is inevitably narrow. But as we progress in this way of life and in faith, our hearts will be enlarged, and we shall run in the way of God's commandments with an inexpressible delight of love. Let us then never swerve from his instructions but rather persevere in God's teaching in the monastery until death. Thus shall we share by patience in the sufferings of Christ, and so deserve also to share in his kingdom. Amen.

RB, prologue.

The character of the abbot

To be worthy of the task of governing a monastery, an abbot must always remember what his title signifies and act accordingly. He is believed to hold the place of Christ in the monastery . . . Therefore, he should never teach or decree or command anything that deviates from the law of the Lord. On the contrary, everything he teaches and commands should, like the leaven of divine justice, permeate the minds of his disciples . . . He ought to lead the community by a two-fold teaching: he must demonstrate to them all that is good and holy, by example rather than by words. He should expound the commandments of the Lord to receptive disciples with words, and demonstrate God's instructions to the stubborn and slow-witted by a living example . . .

The abbot should avoid all favouritism in the monastery. Let him not love one more than another, unless he find someone better in good works and obedience. One born free is not to be given a higher status than one born a slave, except for some other good reason. Nevertheless, the abbot is free, if he sees fit, to alter someone's order in the community as justice demands. Ordinarily, however, all are to observe their customary places because 'whether we are slave or free-born, we are all one in Christ'[22] and all of us alike serve in the army of the same Lord, for 'God shows no partiality among people.'[23] Only in this are we distinguished in God's sight: if we are found better than others in good works and in humility. Therefore, the abbot is to show an equal love to all and apply the same standard of discipline . . .

In his teaching, the abbot should always observe the apostle Paul's advice in which he says: 'Use argument, appeal, reprimand.'[24] In other words, he must display flexibility in his approach, threatening and cajoling by turns, sometimes stern as a taskmaster, at other times devoted and tender as a father. With the undisciplined and truculent, he will need to use firm argument; with the obedient, the sensitive and patient, he will need to encourage them to greater virtue. As for the negligent and contemptuous, we charge the abbot to use reprimand and rebuke. He should not gloss over the sins of those who are at fault, but root them out as soon as they begin to sprout . . .

Once elected, the abbot should always bear in mind what an office he has undertaken and to whom he must 'render an account of his stewardship.'[25] He should remember that it is his duty to profit his community rather than to preside over it. He ought, therefore, to be learned in the divine law so that he can have a treasury of knowledge from which 'he can bring out things both new and old.'[26] Let him be chaste, temperate, and merciful. He should always 'allow mercy triumph over judgement',[27] that he may receive mercy himself. Let him, therefore, hate the sin but love the brothers. When he is forced to punish someone, let him always act with prudence and moderation, lest being too zealous in removing the rust, he end up breaking the vessel. Let him always be conscious of his own frailty and remember that 'a bruised reed is not to be crushed'.[28] In saying this, we do not mean that he should allow vices to flourish. On the contrary, as we have said already, he should eradicate them prudently but gently, in the way which seems best in each case. It should be his aim to be loved rather than to be feared.

Let the abbot not be restless or anxious, not overbearing or obstinate, jealous or overly suspicious, because otherwise he will never be at rest. Instead let him be prudent and considerate in his commands; and regardless of whether the matter concern God or the world, let him always be discerning and moderate, bearing in mind the discretion of holy Jacob who said, 'If I cause my flocks to be overdriven, they will all perish in a single day.'[29] So, taking to heart these and other examples of discretion, the mother of virtues, let the abbot so regulate things that the strong may have something to strive for, and the weak may not draw back in alarm.

RB, 2 and 64.

Making decisions in community

When anything important has to be decided in the monastery, the abbot should call together the entire community and set forth the matter for consideration. When he has heard the advice of the community, he should give it consideration and then judge what seems to be the best course of action. Now the reason why we have said that everyone should be called to counsel, is that God often reveals what is the best course to the younger.

For their part, let the members of the community give their advice with all respect and humility, and not venture to defend their opinions obstinately. The decision, however, should depend on the abbot's judgement, and all should be united in obedience to what he considers prudent. But just as it is fitting for disciples to obey their teacher, so equally it is incumbent upon the teacher to ensure that all things are settled with prudence and justice.

RB, 3.

The Work of God

The psalmist says: 'Seven times a day have I praised you.'[30] We will fulfil this sacred number of seven if we satisfy our obligations of service at Lauds, Prime, Terce, Sext, None, Vespers and Compline . . . Of the night office, it is also written in the psalms: 'At midnight I arose to give you praise.'[31] At these times, therefore, let us praise our Creator 'for the judgements of his justice.'[32] . . . We believe that God is present everywhere, and that 'the eyes of the Lord are in every place, keeping watch on the good and the evil.'[33] But let us particularly believe this without any shadow of doubt when we are engaged in the Work of God. We should be mindful of the psalmist's words : 'Serve the Lord with awe.'[34] And again, 'Sing wisely.'[35] And yet again, 'In the presence of the angels I will sing to you.'[36] We must, therefore, consider how we should behave in the presence of God and his angels, and so sing the psalms that our minds are in harmony with our voices . . .

If we ever wish to bring a matter to the attention of someone powerful, we do so humbly and respectfully for fear of presumption. How much more then should we present our petitions to the Lord God of all things with true humility and purity of intention. We should also remember that we will not be heard for our much speaking, but rather for the purity of our heart and our tears of compunction.[37] Prayer, therefore, should be short and pure, unless on occasion it be prolonged under the inspiration of divine grace. In community, however, prayer should always be brief; and when the superior gives the sign, all should rise together . . .

The oratory should correspond to its name, and not be used for any other purpose or for storage. When the Work of God has been completed, let everyone leave the oratory in absolute quiet, and let reverence for God reign there so that anyone who may wish to pray alone will not be disturbed by the insensitivity of another. And at other times too, if any wish to pray privately, then let them just go in and pray: not in a loud voice, but with tears and fervour of heart.

RB, 16, 19, 20 and 52.

Growing in humility

My brothers, Holy Scripture cries out to us, saying: 'All those who exalt themselves shall be humbled, and all those who humble themselves shall be exalted.'[38] In saying this, the Scriptures are teaching us that all exaltation is a form of pride ... Accordingly, if we wish to reach the summit of humility, if we desire to attain speedily that exaltation in heaven to which we climb by the humility of this present life, then by our ascending actions we must set up that ladder on which Jacob in his dream beheld 'angels descending and ascending.'[39] Such descent and ascent signifies but one thing: we descend by self-exaltation and ascend by humility. Now the ladder erected is our life in this world, and if we humble our hearts, the Lord will raise us to heaven. Now the sides of this ladder are our body and soul, into which our divine vocation has fitted the various rungs of humility and discipline we need to climb ...

When all the various steps in our growth in humility have been climbed, we will reach that perfect love of God which 'casts out fear'.[40] Through this love, all the things which we did more out of fear than anything else, we will now begin to do effortlessly, as though naturally and by habit. We will be motivated no longer by fear of hell, but by our love of Christ, formed by the weight of long practice and a delight in virtue. All this will the Lord, working through the power of the Holy Spirit, graciously manifest in his labourer now purified from vice and sin.

RB, 7.

167

Gifts are for sharing

The vice of personal ownership must be utterly rooted out of the monastery. No one may presume to give or receive anything; no one may claim anything as their own, anything whatever, books, writing tablets, pen, anything at all, without the permission of the abbot; for monks should not have even their own bodies and wills at their own disposal. Rather let all look to the father of the monastery for what they need. It should not be permitted for anyone to have anything which the abbot has not approved. For as Scripture states: 'Let everything be held in common, and let no one claim anything as his own' or treat it as such.[41]

In order that this vice of personal ownership can be rooted out utterly, the abbot is to provide everything that is necessary: that is cowl, tunic, stockings, shoes, belt, knife, pen, needle, handkerchief and writing tablets; so that all pretext of need may be removed. Yet the abbot must always bear in mind the statement in the Acts of the Apostles that 'distribution was made to each according to his need.'[42] So he must bear in mind the weakness of those in need, and ignore the ill-will of the jealous. In all his decisions, furthermore, he must be mindful that God will repay . . .

In advocating that we follow Scripture when it says, 'distribution was made to everyone according to need', we do not imply that favouritism should be countenanced – God forbid – but rather that consideration should be shown for individual weaknesses. Whoever needs less should thank God and not be discontented; and those who need more should feel humble about their weakness, and not self-important on account of the consideration shown to them. In this way all the members of the community will be at peace. Above all, let not the vice of murmuring make an appearance in any word or gesture, for any reason whatever. If anyone is found murmuring, let him undergo severe discipline.

RB, 33 and 55.

In pursuit of a balanced life

Idleness is the enemy of the soul. The brothers, therefore, should have specified periods for manual work, as well as for prayerful reading.[43] ... At the times of study, one or two senior monks should be deputed to go around the monastery to check that there is no brother who is so apathetic that he fritters his time away or is engaged in gossip, thereby neglecting his reading. Not only is he doing himself harm but he is disturbing others as well ...

We believe it to be sufficient for a daily meal ... that there should be available two cooked dishes in consideration of individual dietary needs, so that if some cannot eat one kind of food, they can make their meal out of the alternative. Thus, let two cooked dishes suffice; and if any fruit or fresh vegetables are available, then let a third dish be added. A generous allowance of bread should suffice for the day, some being kept back for supper. If their work is heavier than usual, then the abbot has the choice and power to increase the allowance of food provided that it is appropriate. Above all things, however, let over-indulgence be avoided lest someone suffer from indigestion ... As to drink, we do indeed read that wine is not suitable for monks; but since nowadays monks cannot be convinced of this, let us at least agree to drink moderately and not to excess because 'wine makes even the wise go astray.'[44] ... After the sixth hour, when they have had their meal, let the brothers rest on their beds in complete silence; or if anyone wishes to read by himself, let him read but so as not to disturb the others ...

If the circumstances of the locality or the poverty of the community compels the monks to go and gather the harvest themselves, they should not be discontented; for then are they truly monks when they live by the labour of their hands, as our fathers and the apostles had to. Yet even this is to be done with moderation on account of the faint-hearted ... The abbot should always regulate and arrange things so that souls may be saved and the brothers can go about their work without justifiable murmuring.

RB, 48, 39, 40 and 41.

Keeping Lent

Although the life of a monk ought always to be Lenten in its character, strength for this is found in only a few. Therefore we urge the entire community in these days of Lent to keep their life perfectly pure, and during this holy season to wash away the negligences of former times. This will be worthily done if we guard ourselves against sin, and apply ourselves to prayer with tears, to reading, to compunction of heart and self-denial.

During the days of Lent, let everyone receive a book each from the library which is to read right through from beginning to end. These boooks are to be given out at the beginning of Lent. It is very important that one or two senior monks be appointed to go round the monastery during the time when the brothers are supposed to be reading, to keep an eye on them in case someone may become restless and spend time in idleness or gossip instead of concentrating on his book, thus not only wasting his own time but also disturbing others . . . And let each of us add over and above our usual round of service something by way of private prayer, or abstinence in food or drink. Let each of us offer to God something of our own free will in the joy of the Holy Spirit. We might reduce our diet or the amount we drink, stint ourselves of sleep, curb our talkativeness or joking, all the while looking forward with a joyful spiritual longing to the holy feast of Easter.

Let each person, however, tell the abbot what he is proposing to offer God, and let it be done with his consent and blessing, because what is done without the permission of our spiritual father will be put down to presumption and vanity, and not be reckoned worthy of reward.

RB, 49, part of 48, 49.

Hospitality

Let all guests that come to the monastery be welcomed like Christ, for he will say: 'I was a stranger and you welcomed me.'[45] And let fitting honour be shown to all, but 'especially to those who share our faith'[46] and to pilgrims. As soon, therefore, as guests are announced, let them be met by the superior or by some members of the community, with all the courtesy of love. First of all they should pray together, and thus be united in the kiss of peace ... All humility should be shown to a guest whether on arrival or on departure. By a bow of the head or by the complete prostration of the body, Christ is to be worshipped in them, for indeed he is received in their very persons.[47]

When the guests have been welcomed they should be led to prayer, and then either the superior or someone appointed by him should sit with them. Let the divine law be read to them for their edification, and after this, let every kindness be shown them ... Let the abbot give the guests water for their hands; and let the abbot with the entire community wash their feet. After washing their feet, the community shall recite this verse: 'O God, we have received your mercy in the midst of your temple.'[48] In the reception of poor people and pilgrims special attention should be shown because in them is Christ more truly received; for the fear that the rich inspire is sufficient of itself to secure them respect ...

The guest house should be put in the care of a brother whose soul is full of the fear of God. Let there be a sufficient number of beds ready, and let the house of God be administered by a prudent man in a prudent way.

On no account may any monk who has not been given leave associate with guests or enter into conversation with them. If he meets or sees any, he should greet them humbly as we have said, and after begging a blessing pass on, saying that he is not allowed to talk to a guest.

RB, 53.

Owning our mistakes and failures

If anyone in the course of work, of whatever kind and in whatever place, be it while serving, in the kitchen, in the storeroom, in the bakery, in the garden, while engaged in some craft, or anywhere at all, behave badly, break or lose something, or commit some fault, he should come before the abbot and the community, and of his own accord admit his fault and make satisfaction. If this does not happen, and the fault becomes known through someone else, then he should receive greater censure.

If, however, the matter be a spiritual concern, let him open his heart to his abbot alone, or to a spiritual elder; because they know how to heal both their own wounds and the wounds of others without disclosing and broadcasting the matter to others.

RB, 46.

Meeting with contradictions and injustice

If it should happen that something hard or altogether impossible be asked of a brother, let him accept the command of his superior with complete calm and obedience. But if he perceives that the weight of the burden quite exceeds the limits of his strength, then at an appropriate moment he should explain patiently to his superior the reasons why he cannot do it. Let him never speak in a proud way, or in a spirit of obstinacy or contentiousness. If, after his explanation, the superior still requires him to do what he had originally ordered, then the brother should know that this is what is best for him, and he should obey out of love, trusting in the help of God . . .

We take another step in our growth in humility when in the act of being obedient to what has been laid upon us, we encounter difficulties and contradictions, and even injustice, and meet them with a quiet mind and with a firm grip on patience. In such endurance a person should neither grow faint nor run away, bearing in mind the words of Scripture: 'The one who perseveres to the end will be saved,'[49] and again, 'Let your heart take courage and hope in the Lord.'[50]

Furthermore, to demonstrate how the true disciple ought to endure everything, however painful, for the Lord's sake, Scripture says in the person of those who suffer: 'For your sake do we face death all the day long. We are reckoned no better than sheep marked down for slaughter.'[51] Then, confident of their hope of the divine reward they continue joyfully, saying: 'But in all these things we are more than conquerors through him who loved us.'[52] And again in another place Scripture states: 'O God, you have put us to the test; you have refined us in the fire like silver; you have led us into a snare and have bowed our backs with troubles.'[53] And to show that we ought to be under a superior, it continues: 'You have set others over our heads.'[54]

In truth, those who are patient in the face of hardships and unjust treatment , are fulfilling the Lord's teaching. 'When struck on one cheek, they offer the other. When robbed of their tunic, they surrender their cloak as well. When forced to go a mile, they go two.'[55] And like the apostle Paul, they put up with false brothers and sisters, and 'bless those who curse them.'[56]

RB, 68 and 7.

173

Good zeal

Just as there is an evil zeal rooted in bitterness which separates from God and leads to hell, so there is a good zeal which separates from evil and leads to God and eternal life. This, then, is the good zeal which monks should practise with the most ardent love. 'They should each try to be first in showing respect for another.'[57] They should bear with the greatest patience one another's weaknesses, whether of body or character. They should rival each other in showing mutual obedience. Nobody should follow what seems good for himself, but rather what is best for someone else. Among themselves, they should demonstrate a love born of brotherly affection. Let them fear God. Let them love their abbot with a sincere and humble affection. Let them prefer nothing whatever to Christ. And may Christ bring us all alike to everlasting life.

RB, 72.

Benedict: the man of God

Long before the night office began, Benedict the man of God was standing at his window, where he watched and prayed while the rest of the community were still asleep. In the dead of night he suddenly beheld a flood of light shining down from above more brilliant than the sun, and with it every trace of darkness cleared away. Another remarkable sight followed. According to his own description, the whole world was gathered up before his eyes in what appeared to be a single ray of light . . .

How is it possible for anyone to see the whole universe at a glance? . . . All creation is bound to appear small to a soul that sees the Creator. Once it beholds a little of God's light, it finds all creatures small indeed. The light of holy contemplation enlarges the mind in God until it transcends the world. In fact, the soul that sees God rises even above itself, and as it is drawn upward in God's light all its inner powers unfold. Then, when it looks down from above, it understands how limited everything really is that before had seemed beyond its grasp . . . Why should it surprise us, then, that [Benedict] should have seen the whole world gathered up before him after this inner light had transported him so far above this world? Of course, in saying that the world was gathered up before his eyes, I do not mean that heaven and earth contracted, but rather that his spirit was enlarged. Absorbed as he was in God, it was now easy for him to see all that lay beneath God . . .

Six days before he died Benedict gave orders for his tomb to be opened. Almost immediately, he was seized with a violent fever that rapidly wasted his remaining energy. Each day his condition grew worse until finally, on the sixth day, he had his disciples carry him into the chapel where he received the body and blood of our Lord to gain strength for his approaching end. Then, supporting his weakened body on the arms of his brethren, he stood with his hands raised to heaven and as he prayed breathed his last.

That day two monks, one of them at the monastery, the other some distance away, received the very same revelation. They both saw a magnificent road covered with rich carpeting and glittering with thousands of lights. From his monastery it stretched eastward in a straight line until it reached up into heaven. And there in the brightness stood a man of majestic appearance, who asked them, 'Do you know who passed this way?' 'No,' they replied. 'This,' he told them, 'is the road taken by blessed Benedict, the Lord's beloved, when he went to heaven'. . . And his body was laid to rest in the Chapel of St John the Baptist, which he had built to replace the altar of Apollo.

Gregory the Great, *Dialogues*, II, 35 and 37; ET, Zimmermann and Avery, pp.71-6.

NOTES

1   Gregory the Great, *Dialogues*, II, prologue.
2   *RB*, 73.
3   Gregory the Great, *op.cit.*, II, 36.
4   *RB*, 43.
5   John 6: 28, 29. Prayer is a participation in God's redeeming work in Christ. On derivation of term, see I.Hausherr, 'Opus Dei', *Orientalia Christiana Periodica* 13, 1947, pp.195-218.
6   *RB*, 2.
7   etymologically related to *obaudire* – 'to listen carefully'.
8   *RB*, 48.
9   *RB*, 31.
10 Romans 13: 11.
11 Psalm 95: 8.
12 Revelation 2: 7.
13 Psalm 34: 12; John 12: 35.
14 Psalm 34: 13.
15 Psalm 34: 14, 15.
16 Isaiah 58: 9.
17 1 Thessalonians 2: 12.
18 Matthew 7: 24, 25.
19 Romans 2: 4.
20 Ezekiel 33: 11.
21 In the Latin of the sixth century, *schola* (school) denoted not only a place where instruction was received; it also designated a group receiving instruction: a vocational corporation, people dedicated to the pursuit of a craft or service. Thus, the monastery was a school for holy warfare: 'taking up the strong and glorious weapons of obedience'. Here the background model was possibly that of a gladiatorial school or a military commander with his troops. The monastery was a school of learning: 'listen to the instructions of your teacher'. Here the image was educational. There was the image of the monastery as a household, of a father and his sons: 'attend to the advice of a loving father'; and of brothers together: 'let them practise brotherly love'. No one model was determinative. Benedict presented a cluster of images to underscore the corporate endeavour of the monastery because for him the spiritual life was not a private process. It was a 'school' dedicated to the common good in which the relationship between the abbot and his monks was central. In this Benedict stood in the tradition of cenobitic monasticism.
22 Galatians 3: 28.
23 Romans 2: 11.
24 2 Timothy 4: 2.
25 Luke 16: 2.
26 Matthew 13: 52.
27 James 2: 13.
28 Isaiah 42: 3.
29 Genesis 33: 13.
30 Psalm 119: 164.
31 Psalm 119: 62.
32 Psalm 119: 164.

33 Proverbs 15: 3.
34 Psalm 2: 11.
35 Psalm 47: 8.
36 Psalm 138: 1.
37 on 'compunction' see p.65, n.13; on 'tears' see p.198, n.19.
38 Luke 14: 11; 18: 14.
39 Genesis 28: 12.
40 1 John 4: 18.
41 Acts 4: 32.
42 Acts 4: 35. For Benedict the model of Christian community is the early disciples in Jerusalem where they held everything in common. The abbot is the custodian of the monastery's property.
43 *Lectio divina*: literally, 'divine reading'. In all probability this was exclusively the Bible. For the Fathers, the Bible was a book of mysteries, an encyclopaedia of all knowledge, and thus the highest form of study. Benedict designated optimum times during the day for such reading to make possible a high level of mental alertness. Such reading was not a silent scanning of the page but an actual articulation of the words, which is why he was concerned that no one trying to rest should be disturbed by someone else reading. Monks would repeat the words of the sacred text with their lips so that the body itself entered into the process. They sought to cultivate their capacity to listen to the Word of God at ever deeper levels of inward attention. They borrowed from the vocabulary of digestion to describe this process of ingesting Scripture, and used such expressive terms as *ruminatio* and *mundicare*, the verb to chew the cud. See Beryl Smalley, *The Study of the Bible in the Middle Ages*, 3rd ed. revised, Blackwell, Oxford, 1984.
44 Sirach (Ecclesiasticus) 19: 2.
45 Matthew 25: 35.
46 Galatians 6: 10.
47 The background to this passage is Jesus' parable of the sheep and the goats. The language Benedict uses was not simply that of unconditional welcome, but of worship: Christ is received in every guest and pilgrim. It was seen as a sacramental encounter.
48 Psalm 48: 10.
49 Matthew 10: 22.
50 Psalm 27: 14.
51 Romans 8: 36; Psalm 44: 22.
52 Romans 8: 37.
53 Psalm 66: 10, 11.
54 Psalm 66: 12.
55 Matthew 5: 39-41.
56 2 Corinthians 11: 26; 1 Corinthians 4: 12.
57 Romans 12: 10.

SELECT BIBLIOGRAPHY

TEXTS, TRANSLATIONS and COMMENTARIES

a) The Life of St Benedict

Gregory the Great, *Dialogues*, II, ed. Moricca, Rome, 1924.

The Life and Miracles of St Benedict, ET Odo Zimmermann and Benedict Avery, The Liturgical Press, St John's Abbey, Collegeville, Minnesota, 1981.

b) The Rule of St Benedict

RB 1980: The Rule of St Benedict, ed. T.Fry, The Liturgical Press, St John's Abbey, Collegeville, Minnesota, 1981; in Latin and English; comprehensive study of critical text and commentary.

Numerous other translations are available:

The Rule of St Benedict, in Latin and English; recent reprints only ET, Justin McCann, Sheed and Ward, London and New York, 1952.

Households of God: The Rule of St Benedict, ET David Parry, DLT, London, 1980.

The Rule of St Benedict: A Doctrinal and Spiritual Commentary, Adalbert de Vogue, (ET) Cistercian Publications, Kalamazoo, 1983.

Work and Prayer: The Rule of Benedict for Lay People, ET Catherine Wybourne, commentary Columba Cary-Elwes, Burns and Oates, Tunbridge Wells, 1992.

The Rule of Benedict: Insights for the Ages, ET in inclusive language and commentary by Joan Chittister, St Paul's Publications, Slough, 1992.

BENEDICTINE STUDIES and SPIRITUALITY

de Waal, E, Seeking God: *The Way of St Benedict*, Fount, London, 1984.

de Waal, E, *Living with Contradictions: Reflections on the Rule of St Benedict*, Fount, London, 1989.

McCann, Justin, *Saint Benedict*, rev. ed., Sheed and Ward, London and New York, 1966.

Rees, D., ed., *Consider your Call: A Theology of Monastic Life Today*, SPCK, London, 1978.

8

Gregory the Great
THE DESIRE FOR GOD

'The language of souls is their desire.'
COMMENTARY ON THE BOOK OF JOB

Gregory was born in 540, the son of a Roman senator. His classical education and early governmental career reflected his social status, and in about 573 he became Prefect of Rome. Following the death of his father, Gregory resigned the office, sold his inheritance and gave the proceeds to the poor. He founded six monasteries on family estates in Sicily and converted the family home on the Caelian Hill in Rome into the monastery of St Andrew, where he retired to live as a monk. Years of prayer and study followed, on which he would always look back in nostalgia. He steeped himself in the Scriptures and the Fathers, in particular the writings of Cyprian, Cassian and Augustine. He was ordained deacon and approximately five years later, in 579, was sent by Pope Pelagius II to Constantinople as papal representative to the Patriarch and the Imperial Court.

It was in Constantinople that Gregory delivered various lectures on the Book of Job (which were later edited into a moral commentary). These, together with his later expositions of Scripture (notably his *Homilies on Ezekiel*) provide us with much of his spiritual teaching. This period also saw the beginning of his vast, documented correspondence. In 586 he returned to Rome and withdrew once again to the monastery of St Andrew where he became abbot. In 590, however, following the death of the Pope from the plague, he was elected Pope. During the next fourteen years Gregory was to prove himself an astute administrator and diplomat, securing peace with the Lombards, and friendly relations with the Franks and Visigoths. He sponsored the mission to England, sending monks from his former monastery under the leadership of one called Augustine, who subsequently became the first Archbishop of Canterbury.

During the early years of his pontificate, he produced two more major works. The *Liber Regulae Pastoralis*, the *Book of Pastoral Rule* (or, as it is more commonly known in English, *Pastoral Care*) was written in about 591. The Latin title is significant. The word *regula* by the time of Gregory had acquired an almost technical status: it designated an order of life for a religious community. The most famous example of the use of the term is the *regula* or *Rule* of St Benedict. Gregory was acquainted with this celebrated monastic document, and there is every reason to assume that in conceiving the plan of his own book he intended to provide secular clergy with a spiritual counterpart. His work certainly proved highly influential, and not just with ecclesiastical leaders. It contributed significantly to the formation of the emerging monastic culture of the Middle Ages. Three extracts from it are included in the selection that follows.

The other work of Gregory's early pontificate was the *Dialogues*, written in either 593 or 594. They were a collection of stories compiled to illustrate his conviction that Italy was as capable of nurturing holy women and men as anywhere else. It included a life of Benedict which proved a key factor in the promotion of the Benedictine *Rule*, thereby shaping the future development of Western Christianity. To this early period also belong his collection of *Homilies on the Gospels*. These were principally biblical expositions which emphasised the importance of personal integrity in conduct and lifestyle.

Gregory was not an intellectual. His writings were more general, more broadly based, and tend therefore, to be very accessible to the modern reader. They reveal a cultivated, sensitive man with a strong inner life, having to cope with the burdens of high office at a time of profound unrest. For example, in his *Pastoral Care*, he wrote of the personal stability that was required of a spiritual leader: 'While he is preoccupied with exterior matters, he must not lessen his solicitude for the inner life. Nor when he is preoccupied with his inner life should he relax his watch on exterior concerns. Otherwise, by being engrossed in the pressing duties that assail him, he will experience an interior collapse; or by keeping himself busy solely with things that concern his inner life, he will end up neglecting his external duties to his neighbours.'[1] It is clear from his writings that Gregory suffered poor health for much of his life. This may have been stress-related, but was probably caused (at least in part) by the austerities of his monastic formation. When Gregory wrote of pain and suffering, he wrote from personal experience and not from theory, but never in an oppressive or gloomy way. His words were always measured, breathing a quiet serenity: 'Amid the tumult of outward cares, inwardly a great peace and calm is reigning in love.'[2] People recognised in Gregory a quality of discretion and humanity that continue to be both attractive and authoritative.

Gregory's works were pastorally oriented. As a monk, he had learned the daily discipline of reading and reflecting on Scripture (*lectio divina*).[3] Cumulatively, this had equipped him with a vast Biblical knowledge. In his writings he endeavoured to share this knowledge with his people, and to interpret the Scriptures in such a way as to deepen their desire for God and raise their sights to the threshold of heaven. For Gregory, contemplation was both the fruit of reflection upon the Word of God in Scripture, and at the same time, the gift of God. It was the knowledge of God impregnated with love. He considered that although our active life ceases when we die, our contemplative life which begins here will be perfected in heaven. Contemplation is a resting in God; and in this resting or stillness the mind and heart no longer actively seek God, but instead begin to experience, to taste, what they had been seeking. It places a person in a state of tranquillity[4] and profound interior peace because God is peace. Contemplation for Gregory, therefore, was not simply a way of prayer, it was a way of life, something to be desired for its own sake because it was the life of heaven.

Gregory enjoyed drawing contrasts in theology: presence and absence, possession and dispossession, certainty and uncertainty, active and contemplative, light and darkness, faith and eternal life. The Christian life, for example, he conceived of as a life of detachment and desire: detachment from ourselves, from the world, from success, from sin; and desire for God who alone can satisfy our needs. Desire, for Gregory, was a metaphor for our journey into God. Indeed, it was the theological fulcrum around which his entire spirituality pivoted. Gregory regularly used such words as *anhelare* (to pant, to desire fervently), *aspirare* (to breathe), and *suspirare* (to sigh or long for). Almost all the later spiritual vocabulary of the West had its origin in this evocative language which was itself a re-writing of the vocabulary of Cassian and Augustine.

Spiritual longing is part of our identity as human beings, and it was Gregory's view that such longing propels us inwards to our deepest selves, engaging our will at levels not normally accessible to our conscious minds, particularly at moments of confusion or desolation in our lives when the desires of our hearts are in chaos. He believed that if our desire for God is sincere, then it will also be patient, and will deepen with time and trial. We must learn to wait for God in order to love God more truly. The more intense our desire becomes, the more it will be rewarded by certain possession of God which in turn serves to increase its ardour. 'You know, I say, not through faith, but through love.'[5] 'When we love heavenly realities, we begin to know what we already love, because our love is itself a way of knowing.'[6] Gregory's spirituality was generated by this intense dynamic of love and desire: God awakens our desire, sets it free, and draws it to himself.

Gregory died on 12 March in the year 604. He was sixty-four. As Pope of Rome, he had styled himself 'Servant of the servants of God' – a title that originated with him, and which more than anything else, typified both his personality and his ministry. He entirely deserved the title his epitaph bestowed: 'The Consul of God'.

A servant of the servants of God

The prophet Ezekiel, whom the Lord sent to preach his Word, is described as a watchman.[7] A watchman always selects a high vantage point in order to be able to observe things better. In the same way, whoever is appointed watchman to a people should live on the heights so that he can help his people by having a broad perspective. I find it hard to make such a statement because such words are reproach to myself. My preaching is mediocre, and my life does not cohere with the values I preach so inadequately. I do not deny that I am guilty, for I recognise in myself lethargy and negligence. Perhaps my very awareness of my failings will gain me pardon from a sympathetic judge.

When I lived in a monastic community I could keep my tongue from idle chatter and devote my mind almost continually to the discipline of prayer. However, since assuming the burden of pastoral care, I find it difficult to keep steadily recollected because my mind is distracted by numerous responsibilities. I am required to deal with matters affecting churches and monasteries, and often I must judge the lives and actions of individuals. One moment I am required to participate in civil life, and the next moment to worry over the incursions of barbarians. I fear these wolves who menace the flock entrusted to my care. At another time I have to exercise political responsibility in order to give support to those who uphold the rule of law; I have to cope with the wickedness of criminals, and the next moment I am asked to confront them, but yet in all charity.

My mind is in chaos, fragmented by the many and serious matters I am required to give attention to. When I try to concentrate and focus my intellectual resources for preaching, how can I do justice to the sacred ministry of the Word? I am often compelled by virtue of my office to socialise with people of the world and sometimes I have to relax the discipline of my speech. I realise that if I were to maintain the inflexible pattern of conversation that my conscience dictates, certain weaker individuals would simply shun my company, with the result that I would never be able to attract them to the goal I desire for them. So inevitably, I find myself listening to their mindless chatter. And because I am weak myself, I find myself gradually being sucked into their idle talk and saying the very things that I recoiled from listening to before. I enjoy lying back where beforehand I was conscious lest I fall myself.

Who am I? What kind of watchman am I? I do not stand on the pinnacle of achievement; I languish in the pit of my frailty. And yet although I am unworthy, the creator and redeemer of us all has given me the grace to see life whole and an ability to speak effectively of it. It is for the love of God that I do not spare myself in preaching him.

Homilies on Ezekiel, 1, 11, 4-6.

On preaching

M y dear brothers and sisters, our Lord and Saviour teaches us sometimes through what he says, and sometimes through what he does. For his deeds are precepts in themselves, because when he does something, even without commenting upon it, he is showing us what we ought to do. For example, he sends out his disciples in pairs to preach, because the precepts of charity are two-fold: to love God and to love one's neighbour . . . Our Lord sent out his disciples to preach two by two thereby implying, albeit tacitly, that someone who has no love for people should never take on the task of preaching.

The statement that [the Lord] 'sent them before his face into every city and place where he himself was to come'[8], is very true. For our Lord follows in the wake of those who preach him: preaching paves the way, and then our Lord himself comes to make his home in our souls. Initially we hear words to challenge us, and through their agency our minds become receptive to the truth. It was for this reason that through the mouth of Isaiah preachers are commanded to: 'Prepare the way of the Lord; make straight in the desert the paths of our God.'[9] . . .

[In the Gospel] our Lord declares that his mother and family are not those who are related to him by blood, but rather those who are united to him spiritually. He says: 'Who is my mother and who are my brothers? Those who do the will of my heavenly Father, they are my brother and my sister and my mother.'[10] We should not be shocked that Jesus calls those who do the will of his Father his sisters and brothers because both sexes are included in the faith. But we may be surprised that he should call them his mother as well. How is it that someone who becomes Christ's brother or sister through faith, can also become his mother? We should understand by this that a person who becomes Christ's brother or sister by believing, becomes his mother by preaching. Those who preach Jesus are giving birth to him, as it were, because they are introducing him into the hearts of their hearers. Preachers become Jesus' mother if their words give birth to the love of the Lord in the hearts of their neighbours.

Homily 17 on the Gospels, 1.
Homily 3 on the Gospels, 1.

Scripture: a mirror with which to see ourselves

Holy Scripture confronts the eye of our mind like a mirror in order that we may see our inward face in it. It is there that we come to know both our ugliness and our beauty. In it we can tell what progress we are making and how far we actually are from real improvement. Holy Scripture records the good deeds of the saints and encourages the faint-hearted to emulate them. For just as it records their successes, so it also underscores our frailty in our own struggles with vice. But its words have the effect that our mind is less perturbed in its conflicts because it has the victories of so many brave people set before it.

Sometimes, however, Holy Scripture not only records the victories of the saints, but also their defeats, so that we can learn both from their failures what we ought to be afraid of, and from their triumphs what we ought to aim at imitating. For example, Job is described as raised up by temptation, whereas David is represented as humiliated by it.

In this way our hopes may be nourished by the bravery of those in the past and, by virtue of their frailty, we may be clothed in the armour of humility.[11] The victories of the saints give our spirits wings[12] through the joy they inspire; their failures give us pause for reflection through fear. From Scripture then, we learn both the confidence of hope and the humility of fear.

Commentary on the Book of Job (Moralia), **2, 1, 1.**

In the world but not of the world

My friends, I would like to advise you to leave all earthly goods, but I do not want to sound presumptuous. So if you cannot abandon everything that the world offers, then at least hold the things of this world in such a way that you are not held by them. Earthly goods must be possessed; do not let them possess you. The things that you own must be under the control of your mind. Otherwise, if your mind is dominated by the love of earthly things, you will become possessed by your own possessions.

Let temporal possessions be what we use, eternal things what we desire. Let temporal goods be for use on the way, eternal goods be desired for when we arrive at our journey's end. As regards the business of this world, we should view it obliquely, with a detachment. Let the eyes of our minds gaze straight ahead of us, their attention focused on the destination for which we are bound. Our faults must be torn up by the roots, eradicated not simply from our behaviour but also from the meditation of our hearts. The pleasures of the flesh, the anxieties of life,[13] the fever of ambition must not be allowed to hold us back from the great supper of the Lord. We must even practise a holy indifference with regard to those honourable things which we do in the world, so that the earthly things which delight us may always serve our body and not distract our heart.

My brothers and sisters, I do not presume to tell you to give up everything. Instead I am suggesting that even while retaining your possessions, you can if you wish, let go of them, by so handling temporal matters that you continue to strive with the whole of your mind after eternal aims ... With such an attitude, people are able to use this world as if they had no use for it, bringing to the service of their lives only that which is necessary while never allowing materialism to dominate them. All worldly concerns are under control, serving a person externally, as it were, and never deflecting the concentration of the mind as it aspires to higher things. Those who act in this way have earthly things for their use but not as objects of their desires. They use whatever they need but the sin of avarice is not in them ... So let there be nothing to hold back the desire of your mind; and do not let the delights of this world ensnare you.

Homily 36 on the Gospels, 11-13.

Finding our stability in God

It often happens that immature people,[14] fêted for their good deeds with a flurry of human attention, will end up dissipating themselves in sensuality, and abandoning what they inwardly desire, they become content to wallow in the allurements of this life. Such people delight not so much in becoming holy, as in simply being called holy. And because they crave for applause, they cease to strive after that to which all are called. The net result is that the very means through which they had appeared commendable, now succeeds in alienating them from God.

Sometimes, however, people persevere in good works with a steadfast heart, in spite of being exposed to the ridicule of others. They achieve great things but secure only abuse; and instead of being encouraged to come out of themselves, they are hurt by the insults that are their lot, and are driven in upon themselves. And yet, because they find nowhere to rest in peace, they discover their stability in God, for all their hope is fixed in their creator. In the midst of ridicule and abuse, they become dependent on God, their interior witness. They find themselves estranged to human esteem, but at the same time and in direct proportion, through their distress they are becoming God's neighbour. They pour out their soul to God in prayer and, although hard-pressed on every side, they are being purged inwardly and so enter ever more deeply into their interior world. It is well said [in the Book of Job]: 'Those who are mocked by their neighbours as I am, will call upon God and God will answer them.' For though the wicked may reproach the soul of the good, yet the good are demonstrating whom to seek, the One who witnesses all our endeavours. Through compunction[15] and prayer, the souls[16] of the good are strengthened, and in the very process which had alienated them from the approval [of the world] they are united within themselves in the presence of the Most High.

Commentary on the Book of Job (Moralia), 10, 47, 8.

Make perfect your will

The kingdom of God has no assessed value. It is worth everything you have. To Zacchaeus, it was worth half his possessions; the other half he kept back in order to restore fourfold anything that he had taken unjustly. To Peter and Andrew, it was worth their nets and boat. To the widow, it was worth two small coins. To someone else it is worth a cup of cold water.[17] As I have said, the kingdom of God is worth everything you have. Think about it, my friends. There is nothing cheaper when you go and buy it, and nothing more valuable once you have it.

But suppose you do not have even a cup of cold water to offer someone who needs it? Even then God's Word reassures us. When our Redeemer was born, heavenly voices cried out, 'Glory to God in the highest, and peace on earth to people of good will.' In the sight of God no hand is ever empty of a gift if the heart is filled with good will. The Psalmist says, 'The offerings of praise I will make you, O God, are in me.'[18] He means that although you have no outward gift to offer, you can find within yourself something to place on the altar of God's praise. God has no need of anything we can give, and is better pleased with the offering of our hearts.

There is nothing we can offer to God more precious than our good will. But what is good will? To have good will is to experience concern for someone else's adversities as if they were your own; to give thanks for our neighbour's prosperity as for our own; to believe that another person's loss is our own, and also that another's gain is ours; to love a friend in God, and to bear with an enemy out of love; to do to no one what we do not want to suffer ourselves, and to refuse to no one what we rightly want for ourselves; to choose to help a neighbour who is in need, not only to the whole extent of our ability, but even beyond our means. What offering is richer, what offering is more substantial than this one? What we are offering to God on the altar of our hearts is the sacrifice of ourselves!

Homily 5 on the Gospels, 3-4; ET Leinenweber, pp.64-5.

The gift of patience

Our Lord in the Gospel says, 'By your patience you will gain possession of your lives.'[19] Patience is the root and guardian of all the virtues. We gain possession of our lives by patience, since when we learn to govern ourselves, we begin to gain possession of the very thing we are.

True patience consists in bearing calmly the evils that others do to us, and in not being consumed by resentment against those who inflict them. Those who only appear to bear the evils done them by their neighbours, who suffer them in silence while they are looking for an opportunity for revenge, are not practising patience, but only making a show of it. Paul writes that 'love is patient and kind'.[20] It is patient in bearing the evils done to us by others, and it is kind in even loving those it bears with. Jesus himself tells us: 'Love your enemies, do good to those who hate you; pray for those who persecute you and speak all kind of calumny against you.'[21] Virtue in the sight of others is to bear with those who oppose us, but virtue in God's sight is to love them. This is the only sacrifice acceptable to God.

But often we appear to be patient only because we are unable to repay the evils we suffer from others. As I have said, those who do not pay back evil only because they cannot are not patient. We are not looking to have patience on the surface, but in the heart.

Homily 35 on the Gospels, 4-6; ET Leinenweber, pp.50-1.

Praying for our enemies

When our hearts are reluctant we often have to compel ourselves to pray for our enemies, to pour out prayer for those who are against us. Would that our hearts were filled with love! How frequently we offer a prayer for our enemies, but do it because we are commanded to, not out of love for them. We ask the gift of life for them even while we are afraid that our prayer may be heard. The Judge of our souls considers our hearts rather than our words. Those who do not pray for their enemies out of love are not asking anything for their benefit.

But suppose they have committed a serious offence against us? Suppose they have inflicted losses on those who support them, and have injured them? Suppose they have persecuted their friends? We might legitimately keep these things in mind if we had no offences of our own to be forgiven.

Jesus, who is our advocate, has composed a prayer for our case and in this case the one who pleads our case is also our judge. There is a condition he has inserted in the prayer he composed which reads: 'Forgive us our debts, as we also forgive our debtors.' Since our advocate is the one who comes to be our judge, he is listening to the prayer he himself composed for our use. Perhaps we say the words: 'Forgive us our debts, as we also forgive our debtors,' without carrying them out, and thus our words bind us more tightly; or perhaps we omit the condition in our prayer, and then our advocate does not recognise the prayer which he composed for us, and says to himself: 'I know what I taught them. This is not the prayer I gave them.'

What are we to do then, my friends? We are to bestow our love upon our brothers and sisters. We must not allow any malice at all to remain in our hearts. May Almighty God have regard for our love of our neighbour, so that he may pardon our iniquities! Remember what he has taught us: 'Forgive, and you will be forgiven.' People are in debt to us, and we to them. Let us forgive them their debts, so that what we owe may be forgiven us.

Homily 27 on the Gospels, 8-9; ET Leinenweber, pp.66-7.

Contemplation and the desire for God

It is not our words that make the stronger impression on the ears of God, but our desires. For example, if we seek eternal life with our lips, but do not really desire it with our heart, then although we may be crying out to God in our prayer, in reality we are silent. On the other hand, if we desire [God] with our heart, then even if our lips are silent, in our silence we will be crying out to God. This is why our Lord says in the Gospel: 'When you pray, go into your inner room, shut the door, and pray to your Father who is in secret. And your Father who sees what is done in secret will reward you.'[22] For, when the door is shut and someone is praying in private, what is meant is that though the lips may be silent, the person is pouring out the affection of their heart in the sight of the divine mercy. Thus our voice is heard in secret when it cries out to God in silence with holy desires.

Commentary on the Book of Job (Moralia), 22 ,17, 43.

In the splayed windows [of the temple in Ezekiel's vision] the external part through which the light enters is only a narrow slit, but the interior part that receives the light is wide. Similarly, the souls of those who contemplate see only a feeble glimmer of true light, and yet everything within them expands . . . What they glimpse of eternity in their contemplation is miniscule, but it is sufficient to expand their inward vision, and deepen their desire and love. They receive the light of truth as if spying through a keyhole, and yet everything within them is transfigured.

Homilies on Ezekiel, 2,5, 17.

Searching for the risen Christ

Mary Magdalen[23] had been a 'sinner in the city'.[24] She loved Jesus, the Truth, and washed away the stain of her wickedness with her tears. In this way the word of Truth was fulfilled: 'her many sins have been forgiven her because she has shown great love.'[25] Her sins had chilled her heart, but now she was burning inside with an unquenchable love. When she came to the tomb and did not find the Lord's body, she imagined that it had been taken away, and she went and reported it to the disciples. They came, and saw, and they believed that it had actually happened as she had told them. The Gospel narrative continues: 'The disciples went away again to their homes. But Mary stayed behind, standing by the tomb, weeping.'[26]

At this point let us pause and reflect upon Mary's state of mind, upon the intense love of this woman who would not leave the Lord's tomb even after the disciples had gone away. She carried on seeking him whom she had not found, weeping as she searched;[27] and ablaze with love, she yearned for him whom she believed had been taken away. Thus it happened that she was alone when she saw him, she who had stayed behind to seek him. At the heart of every good work is to be found the virtue of perseverance. Indeed, the lips of Truth itself have said: 'Those who persevere to the end will be saved.'[28]

Mary, 'as she was weeping, stooped down and looked into the tomb.' She had already seen that the tomb was empty and she had told the disciples that the Lord had been taken away; so why did she stoop down again? Why did she want to look a second time? The truth is that it is never enough for a lover to look merely once; the sheer intensity of love will not allow a lover to give up searching. Mary had already sought and found nothing. But she persevered, and therefore found the object of her love. While she was seeking, her unfulfilled desires grew stronger and stronger until at their most intense moment they were quenched in the embrace of him whom she sought.

Holy desires grow with waiting: if they fade through waiting they are not genuine.[29] This must be the quality of love that inflames anyone who reaches out for the truth. It is why David says [in the psalms]: 'My soul is thirsting for the living God; when shall I come and behold the face of God?' And the Church says in the Song of Songs: 'I am wounded by love', and again, 'My soul faints within me.'[30]

'Woman, why are you weeping? Whom do you seek?' She is asked the cause of her sorrow so that her desire may increase, for when she names the one she seeks, she burns with yet greater love for him. 'And Jesus said to her: "Mary".' First of all he called her 'woman', the common address at that

192

time for one of her sex, and she did not recognise him. Then he called her by her own name, as if to say: 'Recognise the one who recognises you.' To Moses the Lord had said: 'I know you by name.'[31] Moses was his own name. The Lord told him that he knew him by name, as if saying to him: 'I do not know you in some general way, but personally.' Addressed by her own name, Mary recognised her creator and immediately calls him 'Rabboni', that is 'Teacher'. Outwardly, it was he who was the object of her search, but inwardly it was he who was teaching her to search for him.

Homily 25 on the Gospels, 1-5.

The goals and pitfalls of spiritual leadership

It is vital that a leader should be studiously vigilant to ensure that he is not motivated by the desire to please people. It is vital that while attending with utmost seriousness to his inner life, and at the same time making sure that all legitimate external matters are also being attended to, a leader should not seek to be loved by his people more than he seeks truth. Otherwise, while relying on his good deeds and securing for himself the appearance of a stranger to this world, the reality of his self-love will render him a stranger to his Creator.

A leader is an enemy to his Redeemer if on the strength of the good works he performs, he desires to be loved by the Church more than by Christ; indeed, such a servant is guilty of adulterous thinking. Although in truth it is the bridegroom who sends gifts through his servant to his bride, the servant is busy trying to secure the eyes of the bride for himself. When such self-love captures a leader's mind, it propels him either into inordinate laxity, or into brutal irascibility. From love of himself, the leader's mind becomes lax. When he sees his people sinning, he dares not correct them because he is frightened their love for him will be weakened; even worse, rather than reprove them, he will actually go so far as to gloss over their faults with adulation. It is well said by the prophet [Ezekiel]: 'Woe to those who sew cushions under every elbow, and make pillows for the heads of people of every age to catch souls.'[32] To put cushions under every elbow is to indulge with smooth flattery souls that are no longer upright, but are reclining in the pleasures of this world. It is as if a person reclined with a cushion under the elbow, or a pillow under the head, when censure is withheld if he sins. In its place is bestowed a deadening favouritism: the sinner reclines at ease in his error because no sharp rebuke has been given.

Of course, leaders will only display such an attitude to those of whom they are frightened, those whom they think can wreck their pursuit of temporal glory. By contrast, folk who (in their estimation) cannot harm them, they constantly hound with bitter and harsh words. Incapable of admonishing such people gently, they abandon any pretence of pastoral sensitivity, and terrify them into submission by insisting on their right to govern. The divine word rebukes such leaders when the prophet says: 'You ruled over the people with force and with a high hand.'[33] Such leaders love themselves more than their Creator, and brag of the qualities of their leadership. But they have no real idea about what they should be doing, and are merely infatuated by power. They have no fear of the Judgement that is to come. They glory arrogantly in their temporal power; it gives them a thrill to do what is wrong with no one to restrain them, confident in the lack of opposition.

Those who act in such ways, and expect others to be silent, witness against themselves, for they want to be loved more than the truth, and expect no criticism. Of course, no one in a position of leadership can go through life without sinning; but we should always want truth to be loved rather than ourselves, and should not seek to protect anyone from the truth. We learn from Scripture that Peter willingly accepted the rebuke of Paul,[34] and that David willingly accepted the reprimand of his servant [Nathan].[35] Good leaders who are not trapped by self-love, welcome free and sincere criticism as an opportunity to grow in humility. It is important, therefore, that the gift of leadership should be exercised with the great art of moderation, in order that those in their charge should have freedom of speech and not feel intimidated from expressing an opinion. Of course, such freedom should not become a cause for pride; if liberty of speech be granted too generously, personal humility is in danger of being undermined.

Thus, let it be noted that good leaders should wish to please their people, but always in order to draw their neighbours to the love of truth by the high regard in which they are held. Leaders should not long to be loved for themselves, but should wish that the love of their people should become a sort of road which leads the hearts of their hearers to the love of their Creator. It is difficult for one who is not loved, however well he may preach, to obtain a sympathetic hearing. So let those who lead aim at being loved in order that they may be listened to, but never for their own sake lest it become the root of an inner rebellion of the mind against the One whom publicly in their office they serve.

Pastoral Care, II, 8.

The quality of true Christian leadership

While a leader is preoccupied with exterior matters he must not lessen his solicitude for the inner life. Nor when he is preoccupied with his inner life should he relax his watch on exterior concerns. Otherwise, by being engrossed in the pressing duties that assail him, he will experience an interior collapse; or by keeping himself busy solely with things that concern his inner life, he will end up neglecting his external duties to his neighbours.

Often some leaders, forgetting that they have been given oversight of their brothers and sisters for the sake of their souls, devote the energies of their heart to secular causes. These they gladly attend to as often as occasion demands; but when occasion is not present, they find themselves bereft, hankering after engagements day and night, their minds disoriented and awry. If they discover they have some free time because they have no commitments, they suddenly feel exhausted not through stress, but by the emotional vacuum. The reality of their situation is that they find pleasure in being weighed down by external duties, and find it impossible to stop working. In such circumstances, while they rejoice in being weighed down by the many heavy demands of the world, they neglect their inner life which ought to be the well from which they teach others.

As a direct consequence of this, it is inevitable that the life of their people will languish. Although the people want to make spiritual progress, in the example of their leaders they are confronted by a stumbling-block. As long as the head languishes, the members will degenerate. It is a waste of time for an army, seeking to engage the enemy in battle, to hurry behind its leader if he has lost his way. No exhortation will succeed in raising the minds of people, no rebuke will succeed in amending their faults, if it issues from a spiritual guardian who prefers to be immersed in secular duties: the shepherd's care of the flock will be missing. People cannot see the light of truth, for when secular affairs preoccupy a pastor's mind, dust, driven by the winds of temptation, blinds the eyes of the Church.

Pastoral Care, II, 7.

The integrity of the preacher

It often occurs when a sermon has been delivered well and with a powerful message, that afterwards the mind of the preacher is elated with a sense of joy at his own performance. In such circumstances, take great care to examine yourself rigorously, lest in restoring others to health by healing their inner wounds, you disregard your own inner well-being, and foster the cancer of pride. While helping your neighbour, never neglect to examine yourself; never raise up others, but fall yourself.

In many cases, the very greatness of a preacher's virtue can be the occasion of his downfall because he has felt over-confident in his own ability, and has perished through negligence. Indeed, in the struggle of virtue against vice, the mind can sometimes flatter itself. It is almost as if it becomes exhilarated by the contest with the result that the soul ceases to be cautious or circumspect, and puts its confidence in its own ability to perform well. It is at this juncture that the cunning Seducer infiltrates himself, enumerating to the soul a catalogue of the person's successes, enlarging the ego with conceited thoughts about superiority over others. . . .

This is why it is so important that when a wealth of virtues flatter us, we should turn the eye of our soul to gaze upon our weaknesses, and that for our own good, we should constantly lie in humility before God. We should attend not to the good we have done, but to the good we have failed to do, so that while the heart becomes contrite in recollecting its frailty, it may be the more solidly established in the eyes of the Author of humility. For although almighty God will bring to perfection in large measure the minds of those whose task it is to lead, he will always leave them in some sense unfinished in order that, when they are resplendent in their marvellous achievements, they may still grieve their imperfections; and because they constantly have to struggle over trivial things that plague them, they will not be tempted to over-estimate themselves when confronted by major things. If they cannot overcome the little things of life that afflict them, they will be less likely to pride themselves on the great things they may accomplish.

My good friend,[36] compelled by the urgency of your request, I have tried to set forth for you the qualities of a pastor. I, miserable artist that I am, have painted the portrait of a ideal leader; and here I am, busy pointing others to the shore of perfection, but tossed about myself on the waves of sin. In the shipwreck of this life, sustain me, I beg you, with the plank of your prayers, so that as fast as my weight pulls me below the waves, your meritorious hand may lift me up.

Pastoral Care, IV.

NOTES

1   *Pastoral Care*, I, 7.
2   *Commentary on the Book of Job (Moralia)*, 18, 43, 70.
3   cf., p.177, n.43.
4   see below n.11.
5   *Homily 14 on the Gospels*, 4.
6   *'amor ipse notitia est' – Homily 27 on the Gospels*, 4.
7   Ezekiel 3: 17.
8   Luke 10: 1.
9   Isaiah 40: 3.
10   Matthew 12: 46-50.
11   Active humility is not the acquisition of a principle; it is an experience, a growth in personal awareness. cf. 'Do not take thought in yourself of what you have, but of who you are.' *Homily 28 on the Gospels*, 3.
12   Spiritual flight is one of Gregory's favourite themes. It contrasts with his idea that we are naturally attracted to the earth: our weight, our 'gravity', is a sign of our mortality and sinfulness; sin literally 'drags us down'. But the force of love intensifies our spiritual quest, and a new weight carries the soul toward God, the 'weight of love' which is greater than our present infirmity.
13   Gregory identifies acute anxiety and agitation (*inquietudo*) as symptoms of human malaise and our subjection to the changes and chances of this life. 'We are no longer able to see those objects above us which we were able to see when our mind was calm' (*Commentary on the Book of Job (Moralia)*, 20, 63). We need to develop a tranquil mind, and to foster our desire for God who alone is our peace and our stability. cf. Basil, p.84 , n.6.
14   literally, those of 'weak minds'.
15   Job 12: 4.
16   For Gregory, compunction had a double aspect. It was an experience of pain through the realisation of sin and, at the same time, of our ache for God. More than other writers, Gregory emphasised this latter aspect. Compunction is an act of grace by which God awakens us and stimulates us to deepen our desire for him. cf., p.65 , n.13.
17   Matthew 10: 42
18   Psalm 56: 11.
19   Luke 21: 19.
20   1 Corinthians 13: 4.
21   Luke 6: 27, 28.
22   Matthew 6: 6
23   In this portrayal of Mary Magdalene, Gregory conflated three separate figures: the sinful woman of Luke 7: 36-50, the woman who annointed Jesus in Matthew 26: 7 and Mark 14: 3, who is called 'Mary' in John 12: 3, and Mary Magdalene herself. He meditates on the connection between desire and absence in her search for the risen Christ.
24   Luke 7: 37.
25   Luke 7: 47.
26   John 20: 11
27   The theme of tears often recurs in Gregory's writings. He identifies two types: those of repentance (the lower stream); and those of desire (the higher stream).

> Tears of love always accompany true penitence, and increasingly they are superseded by tears of joy.

28 Matthew 24: 13.
29 It was Gregory's belief that delay purifies our prayer because it purges our motives; waiting humbles us and deepens our need and yearning for God.
30 Song of Songs 2: 5, 5: 6.
31 Exodus 33: 12.
32 Ezekiel 13: 18. The passage in fact refers to pseudo-prophets, those who delude the people through false divination. Gregory applies the text to bishops who allow their people to go astray because they refuse to correct wrong-doing.
33 Ezekiel 34: 4.
34 Galatians 2: 11.
35 2 Kings 12: 7ff.
36 Gregory wrote his treatise for John, bishop of Ravenna; but it is probable that he had composed parts of it earlier while still living at St Andrew's monastery.

SELECT BIBLIOGRAPHY

TEXTS and TRANSLATIONS

PL, 75-79.
Gregorii Magni Dialogi, ed., U. Moricca, Rome, 1924.
Homiliae in Hiezechielem Prophetam, critical ed., M. Adriaen. CCSL, 1971.
Moralia in Iob critical ed., Robert Gillet, SC, Books 1-2 (vol.32); 11-14 (vol.212); 15-16 (vol.221), 1974.
Pastoral Care, ET Henry Davis, ACW 11, Newman Press, New York, 1950.
NPNF 12.
Forty Gospel Homilies, ET David Hurst, Cistercian Publications, Kalamazoo, Michigan, 1980.
Leinenweber, John, *Be Friends with God: Spiritual Reading from Gregory the Great*, ET of selected Gospel Homilies with introduction, Cowley Publications, Cambridge, Mass, 1990; SPCK, London, 1990.

STUDIES and ARTICLES

Butler, E.C., *Western Mysticism*, 3rd ed., Constable, London, 1967; Barnes and Noble, New York, 1968.
Evans, G.R., *St Gregory the Great*, Cambridge, 1986.
Leclercq, John, (ET) *The Love of Learning and the Desire for God*, SPCK, London; Fordham University, New York, 1978.
Richards, Jeffrey, *Consul of God: The Life and Times of Gregory the Great*, Routledge and Kegan Paul, London, 1980.
Straw, Carole, *Gregory the Great: Perfection in Imperfection*, Univ. of California, Berkeley, 1988.
Petersen, J.M., 'The Biblical and Monastic Roots of the Spirituality of Pope Gregory the Great', *Monastic Studies II*, ed., Judith Loades, Headstart History, Bangor, 1991, pp.31-42.
Ward, B, 'Gregory the Great', *The Study of Spirituality*, ed., Jones, Wainwright and Yarnold, SPCK, London, 1986, pp.277-80.

GENERAL BIBLIOGRAPHY

Beatrice, P.F., (ET) *Introduction to the Fathers of the Church*, ed. Istituto San Gaetano, Vicenza, Italy, 1987.
An excellent volume putting the significant figures of the early centuries in context; short, well illustrated and presented

Bouyer, Louis, (ET) *The History of Christian Spirituality I: The Spirituality of the New Testament and the Fathers*, Burns & Oates, Tunbridge Wells, 1968.
A comprehensive reference book: not for the general reader.

Clement, Olivier, (ET) *The Roots of Christian Mysticism*, New City, London, Dublin, Edinburgh, 1993.
An exciting presentation of the spirituality of the Fathers by a leading Orthodox theologian, with an excellent choice of texts.

Comby, Jean, (ET) *How to Read Church History (I) : From the beginnings to the fifteenth century*, SCM, London, 1985.
An ideal introduction; easy to dip into; well presented.

Frend, W.H.C., *The Rise of Christianity*, DLT, London, 1984.
A massive overview of the life and thought of the early Church; a rather heavy read for the uninitiated.

Hamman, Adalbert, (ET) *How to Read the Church Fathers*, SCM, London, 1991.
The companion volume to Jean Comby (see above).

Hazlett, Ian (ed.), *Early Christianity: Origins and Evolution to AD 600*, SPCK, London, 1991.
A good selection of essays on various topics for the serious student.

Jones, Wainwright & Yarnold (eds.), *The Study of Spirituality*, SPCK, London, 1986.
A series of short articles spanning the entire Christian era, covering individuals, topics, contemporary trends; useful reference book.

Louth, Andrew, *The Origins of the Christian Mystical Tradition: From Plato to Denys*, OUP, 1981.
A scholarly analysis but not always an easy read.

McGinn, Meyendorff & Leclercq (eds.), *Christian Spirituality: Origins to the Twelfth Century*, Routledge & Kegan Paul, London, 1986.
A series of substantial articles presented thematically; reference only.

Ramsey, Boniface, *Beginning to Read the Fathers*, DLT, London, 1987.
The teaching of the Fathers presented in a thematic way.

Squire, Aelred, *Asking the Fathers*, SPCK, London, 1994.
A presentation of themes of Christian spirituality geared to the general reader.

INDEX

Lightning Source UK Ltd.
Milton Keynes UK
UKOW05f2338280417
300165UK00001B/118/P